India and the Awakening East

BOOKS BY ELEANOR ROOSEVELT

This Is My Story

This I Remember

India and the Awakening East

INDIA
and the
AWAKENING EAST

by
ELEANOR ROOSEVELT

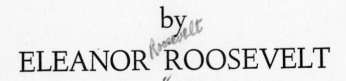

HARPER & BROTHERS, PUBLISHERS

New York

1953

INDIA AND THE AWAKENING EAST

Copyright, 1953, by Anna Eleanor Roosevelt
Printed in the United States of America
By The Haddon Craftsmen, Inc., Scranton, Pa.

Library of Congress catalog card number: 52-7298

Acknowledgments

Every place I went in the travels which are described in this book, there are innumerable people to whom I am deeply grateful for the help they gave me in seeing, learning and appreciating what was happening in their particular country.

My thanks should really begin by recognition of all the co-operation given me in the State Department by the heads of the bureaus in charge of the countries I visited and by their officials. In all the countries we visited our State Department representatives were more than kind.

Every representative of a foreign government was thoughtful beyond words. I think particularly of the government representatives in Lebanon, Syria, Jordan, Israel, Pakistan, India, Thailand, Indonesia and the Philippines. My warm thanks go to them all.

In the preparation of this book, I owe warm thanks to my former secretary, Miss Malvina Thompson, who did a major part of the work before her death; to Miss Maureen Corr and Dr. David Gurewitsch, who went with me on the trip and have been invaluable in helping me remember many details; and to Miss Marguerite Hoyle, who has done a great service in rearranging and editing much of my material.

ELEANOR ROOSEVELT

Contents

ACKNOWLEDGMENTS   V

INTRODUCTION   ix

1 THE ARAB SIDE: LEBANON, SYRIA AND JORDAN   1

2 ISRAEL: A DEDICATED LAND   35

3 AS PAKISTAN SEES IT   50

4 THE KHYBER PASS: A SENTIMENTAL JOURNEY   92

5 THE CHANGING INDIA   101

6 NEPAL   208

7 HOMEWARD BOUND   213

   BY WAY OF CONCLUSION   221

   INDEX   231

Groups of illustrations will be found following pages 46 and 142.

Introduction

"Why do you want to go on this trip? It is going to be fatiguing, and my dear, it may even be dangerous! At your age, why do you want to do it?"

So spoke a solicitous friend of mine when I talked tentatively about accepting the very kind invitation to visit India which Prime Minister Nehru brought me when he came to the United States in 1950. I was even a little older in 1952 when I finally set off on that very rewarding trip. However, aside from the interest I have always had in seeing new countries and new people, new habits and customs, I had a particular reason for wanting to go to that part of the world, a reason born of my experiences in the UN.

Since that invitation was first extended to me, I had seen growing in the United Nations a tendency for nations that are closely joined geographically or by common interests to come together and vote en bloc rather than to consider each question on its merits and to try objectively to understand the opposing point of view. I became conscious of this first during the session of the General Assembly in New York City in the autumn of 1950. In the last Assembly —1951-1952—which met in Paris, this tendency grew and was manifest in several committees. It was particularly evi-

[ix]

dent in the committee on which I served, one that deals with humanitarian, cultural and social matters. Of all the UN committees, Committee Number Three, as it is known, is perhaps the most quickly responsive to people's real feelings; for it is here that questions come up that have an emotional rather than an intellectual appeal. Wise handling would demand the use of both mind and heart; nevertheless decisions were sometimes made on a purely emotional basis rather than as the result of careful study and understanding of all points of view.

In Committee Number Three, feelings ran high over the question of continuing the Children's Emergency Fund, to take one example. During the years of fighting, many of Europe's children had suffered from malnutrition and from lack of medical care. After the war milk was still scarce, so many cows having been killed; crops were also inadequate, since both agricultural implements and fertilizers were unavailable. Moreover, many children were still living in makeshift shelters or partially destroyed houses. Most of us on the Committee knew that once Europe's lands and Europe's economy were even partly restored, she would again feed and house her children properly as she had in the past. In the meantime, to meet the temporary emergency, she needed not only food and clothing and medicines, but cod-liver oil, books, paper, pencils and toys.

The idea of the Children's Emergency Fund as an answer to this need had been suggested by a highly emotional

Introduction

young Norwegian, Mr. Aak Ording. The organization appealed to a great many countries. Mr. Evatt of Australia told me that it was the first organization to make the United Nations come alive to the people of Australia. Here was something they could understand and respond to, and they gave to it more liberally than for any other purpose. By 1951 the emergency in Europe was over; in the meantime, however, the organization had expanded. It had come to the aid of children among the Palestine refugees; it had started some work in the Far East, and in Latin America and in India. Many people felt that it should be continued, if only for the reason that Mr. Evatt had given me—that it provided a human touch that made the United Nations real to people throughout the world.

But something interesting had happened: the people now being reached were people only too familiar with the conditions under which their children had been living; as Mr. Bokhari, the Pakistan representative, put it, life for them was "a constant emergency." The United States Congress was beginning to feel the international drain on the country's resources. It announced that it would give no more money now that the organization had ceased to deal with an emergency, unless the committee would say honestly that this was no longer emergency work. I tried my best to explain to the delegates in Committee Number Three the attitude of our Congress. I explained that these men were representing generous people, they were generous themselves, warmhearted and easily touched, but that they also had a responsibility to their constituents and their country. Taxpayers' money must be expended wisely and the taxpayers must know just what it was being spent for.

I explained painstakingly that we, in the United States, felt it was more honest to face this new situation as a permanent one. The children of the Middle East, the Far East and of some countries in Latin America and Africa have been underfed, ill-clothed and ill-housed for generations. There were now some 575,000,000 of them in this category and even if all the resources of the world were mobilized, the Children's Emergency Fund could not hope to give each child as much as half a cup of milk a day.

Our contention was that this problem must be met by increasing the supply of food in the needy areas. The United States did not maintain that no surpluses should be distributed; but it did state that the emphasis should shift from a program of simply giving out supplies of medicine and food to a program of carrying through, with the aid of the member nations themselves, projects that would increase food supplies and multiply the available technical services—whether the need was for a processing plant or for medical care or for the production of certain medical supplies. Since this would be a long-range as well as a world-wide program, we thought that the administrative expenses should be included in the United Nations budget and that every nation should pay a small share of the administrative burden. We also felt that the new plans must be carried out in conjunction with other specialized agencies. Health projects should be worked out in consultation with the World Health Organization, projects aimed at increasing food supplies should be developed with the advice and help of the Food and Agricultural Organization, those for improving the education of children with UNESCO. Plans for improving child labor laws ought to be made in conjunction with the International Labor Organization.

All of this seemed eminently sensible to me, but Committee Number Three, as I have suggested, is highly emotional, and led by Mr. Bokhari, its members told me in no uncertain terms that we should do for the children of the Middle East and other needy countries exactly what had been done for the children of Europe. An age-old sore had come to light and I felt the weight of history for which the nations of the Western world are now to be called to account.

One day Mr. Bokhari said, "You, Mrs. Roosevelt, do not care what happens to the children of Asia; they are colored. The children of Europe are white." Shades of colonial history, of exploitation in the years gone by, both political and economic! I could not feel that many of us had completely clean hands in the pages of history, nor, while I denied that Mr. Bokhari's statement was true, could I resent his accusations against a system from which the

East had suffered for many years. Now, as members of the United Nations, the countries of Asia felt they could express their feelings openly, for each one of them had an equal vote in any committee with the governments of the Western world.

Dr. Karim Azkoul of Lebanon, during the debate, said something like this: "Mrs. Roosevelt has almost persuaded me, but she does not know my people. For centuries when their children have died they have said: 'It is the will of God.' When their children had been spared they have said: 'It is the grace of God.' Now if perhaps we showed them, by giving them proper food and medical care, that their children need not die, they would turn to their governments and insist that conditions be changed and that their children be given a chance to live in the future."

I remarked that he was expecting a great deal from people who had suffered in the same way for centuries. It has always seemed to me that revolt requires leadership, and a people with sufficient initiative to make demands upon their government in the first place. And this in turn requires a fairly long education in the personal responsibilities of citizenship, and an experience of free speech and association—a background not easily or quickly built up in that part of the world. Nevertheless, the representatives of these nations voted overwhelmingly to set up for three years a Children's Emergency Fund, with the primary object of distributing supplies.

Introduction

Since then the Fund itself has found that of necessity it must change its program, and today is following exactly the course that we in the United States delegation suggested.

In any case, what I mean to bring out is that the awakening of the East was first felt in Committee Number Three in the session of 1950. In 1951 and 1952 the lesson was driven home in committee after committee. I began to feel that we in the United States did not understand what created these tensions and emotions that crackled through the UN and we certainly lacked knowledge of the conditions out of which they grew. It was to gain this understanding, if I could, that I finally decided to accept Prime Minister Nehru's invitation. For as the months passed, the problems grew no fewer, the misunderstandings no less acute. By the time the last session of the Assembly ended on February 6, 1952, there was not a member of the U.S. delegation who had not become aware of the complexity of the difficulties confronting us in Asia. A growing dislike of the foreigner, particularly in the Middle East, was compounded by the feeling that the great powers, with the exception of the Soviet Union and China, whose position was different, belonged to a race that looked down on the other races of the world. Aggravating all this was an acute realization of economic dependence and fear of imperialism. These nations know that they must have aid if they are to accomplish the reforms that they realize their people are

Introduction

beginning to demand. But they dislike the feeling that we do not consider them equals and do not recognize the contributions they not only could make but have made for centuries to the development of civilization.

The people of these countries are realizing it is no longer necessary to live in misery and disease. But they do not want charity. They belong to the United Nations; their vote is as good as that of anyone else; they want what they consider their right—an equal chance to develop to a point where life is worth living.

The question is, where will their awakening lead, and who will guide it? Will communism or democracy be the choice of the awakening East?

India and the Awakening East

1

The Arab Side: Lebanon, Syria and Jordan

By the time I left Paris on my Eastern trip in February, 1952, my schedule had been expanded to include flying visits to Lebanon, Syria, Jordan and Israel, as well as Pakistan and India. The man chiefly responsible for this change was Dr. Charles Malik, the brilliant chairman of the United Nations Committee on Human Rights. Hearing of my plan to go to India, he had begged me to visit also some of the Arab countries, particularly his own, pointing out that I would have to fly over them in any case on my way to India.

It was a welcome suggestion; and so it was arranged that I should spend a fortnight seeing something of some of the Arab countries and Israel, before going on to Pakistan and India.

Maureen Corr, who works with me in my New York office, agreed to accompany me on the trip, and we were to be joined in Jerusalem by Dr. David Gurewitsch, my personal physician, who had long wanted an opportunity to revisit Israel and to see India.

Obviously in the short time I had I could not hope to get deeply beneath the surface of any of these countries or to become in any sense an expert on their problems. Yet I did want to see for myself what the conditions were like and to learn as much as I could about the internal and external problems these people face and—more important perhaps—what and how they thought and felt about them. I think I did gain some understanding; and because what I learned has been helpful to me in forming a clearer picture of the situations our country must deal with in the Middle East and Asia I decided to write out my observations in the hope that others too might find them useful.

One impression I formed almost the moment we landed at the fine modern airport outside Beirut in Lebanon, and it was strengthened as my trip wore on. There was no doubt that the feeling against foreigners, about which many people had warned me, really did exist. Behind the kindness and the courtesy of the government officials—for after all there is no point in being actually rude to the United States or its representatives—I was fully conscious of a certain amount of hostility. One of our own government people who was stationed there cautioned me to remember that the diplomatic gestures of the officials of the Lebanese government did not really represent the attitude of the people as a whole. The Lebanese officials themselves were apparently a little apprehensive, for at first, wherever I went, I was accompanied by a carload of soldiers, and security officers were everywhere. Whenever we stopped even for a moment the soldiers all swarmed out of the car alertly; it was only too evident that they thought I might be unpleasantly received. Though I appreciated the official solicitude for my well-being, I could not bring myself to believe that all these precautions were really necessary and when I finally insisted on dispensing with my armed guard I am afraid they credited me with being either unwarrantably courageous or foolhardy. However, there were no untoward incidents; and I found on the whole, when I actually got out among the people themselves, in their homes and shops, and talked to them singly or in groups, that the atmosphere was friendly and hospitable.

Nevertheless, the dislike, or at best the mistrust, that the people of the Near and Middle East feel toward the West in general—not only the United States—is a reality and it is a reality which we have to take into consideration and try to understand rather than simply resent, if we are to be effective there. Actually it is not hard to understand when one reflects that for literally hundreds of centuries the Arab world has been misruled by wave after wave of conquerors. There were the Egyptians and before them the Phoenicians; after the Egyptians came the Assyrians and Hittites and Persians, Greeks, Romans, Moslems. They were invaded by the Crusaders, the Mongols, and the Mamelukes of Egypt.

Then for four hundred years they were under Turkish rule, until after the First World War, when Lebanon and Syria were made a French mandate and Jordan a British mandate. Lebanon and Syria did not gain complete independence until 1943 and Jordan not until 1946. Lebanon and Syria both adopted a republican form of government with a president and a parliament (though Syria is now ruled by a military junta); Jordan is a kingdom, with a House of Representatives elected by the people and a House of Notables appointed by the king.

Under few of their rulers, I am afraid, was the welfare of the country of much moment, and the people were exploited, impoverished and repressed. With such a history, it is easy to understand how jealous they are of their new but long-dreamed-of independence and why they react so suspiciously to any suggestion of foreign influence.

Understandable though their attitude is, however, it is a tragedy for their own sake as well as for ours. For these countries—with their land depleted, their population growing, their water supplies inadequate—are in desperate need of outside help. When I was there Syria had refused to accept Point Four aid, fearing it would mean economic domination by the United States. Lebanon too was at first suspicious of our motives, but eventually agreed to accept our co-operation and now has an active Point Four program.

Nevertheless, I think whenever a country is reluctant to accept our aid, we would be wiser not to force matters but to hold back and wait until we are asked for help. If we did this, they would be less inclined to worry about the reasons behind our offer. They believe that our objection to communism has much to do with our concern for them, so they cannot believe that our motives are altogether unselfish or disinterested. They do not understand that in our own interest we want to help them achieve a standard of living that will make that part of the world politically stable. Consequently, though they need our help, they are all too often afraid to take it, lest we use our Point Four program to dominate them.

I learned quickly that each of the problems confronting these countries has many aspects; they are all so interconnected that it is impossible to isolate any one of them and deal with it alone. For instance, what hits you in the face wherever you go is the appalling poverty of the people in general—whether peasant or town dweller—a poverty that the average American farmer or worker would find it hard to conceive of. When you try to get at the root of it, you find a combination of causes. For one thing, though the economy of the Arab world is predominantly agricultural, it does not have enough land under efficient cultivation to feed its own people. This in spite of the fact that every possible bit of ground is made use of. Citrus fruits, olives, dates, cereals are the main food products of these countries and one sees them growing in the most unlikely places. The mountains are high and steep but they are terraced

[5]

from top to bottom and cultivated even more assiduously than they are in Switzerland. To an American it is really incredible how every little bit of ground is made to yield some portion of a man's living. On the way to Beit-ed-dine one day, an ancient and beautiful summer palace high in the hills above Beirut, we stopped off to visit briefly with a Lebanese farmer and his family. They welcomed us warmly and invited us into the house, which was meagerly though adequately furnished with pieces that obviously had been gathered one by one over many generations. But I was most interested in his tiny, well-tended mountainside wheat fields. It struck me forcibly how eloquently they bespoke the industry and resourcefulness of these men of the soil. Our host was well-to-do by Lebanese standards, yet he told me that in addition to farming his own place, he had to work by the day for others in order to eke out his family's living.

Part of the trouble is that these countries have still to go through the industrial revolution. Their methods of farming are unbelievably primitive—ploughing for example is done with a stick and oxen, and hand sickles are used in harvesting. In all this area of the world it is men's hands and their beasts of burden that do the work. Modern implements would make a tremendous difference to them, though I can readily see it would be impossible to use our big agricultural machinery on some of these small, steep and rocky fields. The land itself is poor. Centuries of deforestation and overgrazing have resulted inevitably in a cruel erosion of the earth as the rains have carried off the topsoil. Moreover, the region is dry and hot, the rainfall scanty, flood control and irrigation systems few and usually primitive. In some of the villages of Lebanon dams built, I believe, by the Phoenicians are still being used. Indeed, I found lack of water a fundamental problem everywhere I went.

Meanwhile the population of the area is growing, which means that the pressure of the people on the land is increasing. This question of population is one that came up in almost every conversation, for all the government officials as well as the outside experts are keenly aware of its seriousness. Even emigration cannot wholly solve it. Ever since the nineties large numbers of Lebanese have been leaving the country every year; and today, I am told, more of them are living in other countries than in Lebanon itself.

Another factor contributing to the over-all destitution of the Arab countries is of course the high rate of illiteracy. Here Lebanon has the best record of any of the Middle Eastern Arab states—only about a fifth of its people are unable to read and write—whereas in the rest of the Arab countries the rate is around 90 per cent and in the rural areas nearer 95 per cent. What this means is that the peasants are not able to take advantage of the information about new or better methods of agriculture that would otherwise be available to them. If they could read and write, it would be possible to make them understand a great many things, not only about farming but about such matters as sanitation, public health and conservation, that now have to be explained to them by word of mouth, or demonstrated. Industrially, too, the countries of the Middle East desperately need technical assistance from the United States and through the United Nations if they are ever to develop to the point where they can provide employment for their people and raise their standard of living. They have few modern industries; the little they have in the way of mineral resources is largely undeveloped, and there is no hydroelectric power to speak of.

Of the three countries I visited in this area, Jordan was the least advanced and Lebanon the furthest. The Lebanese are and have been since the days of the Phoenicians shrewd traders and merchants. Their principal city, Beirut, is a busy commercial port, accessible both by sea and air, and a favorite stop for cruise ships. I shall never forget my first morning there when I opened my window and looked out on the incredibly beautiful blue harbor and brilliant red beach with the mountains rising steeply behind. The air was soft but it had an exhilarating tang that one does not ordinarily find in a warm climate. Beirut has good hotels, modern steel and concrete apartment houses, telephones that work, trolleys and an enormous number of American-made cars, good French shops and French restaurants. Indeed, the city has a distinctly French feel, and I am told that the French are still active in the business life of the community. Lebanon, it is true, does have a number of new industries. I went through one very modern textile mill in which all the machinery had been brought from England. It was up-to-date in every way, and the workers' health was protected by an efficient air-conditioning system, which sucked the dust particles from the air.

In Syria, too, cotton is an important crop, and the textile industry is growing faster than any other. The mill I visited there was not quite so modern as the one I saw in Lebanon. The machinery came from the United States but there was no air conditioning; however, I was glad to see that the rule requiring the workers to wear masks was being pretty carefully observed.

The crowded covered bazaars of Damascus, which I found fascinating, gave colorful evidence of the enterprise of the Syrians. And the variety and excellence of their gold and silver work, their copper and brass utensils, their leather goods and silks and wood carvings prove that their ancient skills still exist. There's no question that as shopkeepers these people are good. They seem to know instinctively how to buy, how to display, how to sell.

I was not in Jordan long enough to see a great deal, though I crowded in as much as I could. It is, of course, largely desert, except for the fertile western portion which has great agricultural possibilities. Jordan also has some potash and phosphate deposits under development, and surveys for oil are now being made. On the whole, however, both the desert Arabs and the agricultural workers in Jordan only just barely manage to keep alive. And, as I have tried to show, the lot of the average peasant or townsman in Lebanon or Syria is not a great deal better.

As an inevitable corollary, all these countries have a serious unemployment problem. Even in a bustling city like Beirut, with a population of 211,000, there are some 50,000 unemployed white collar workers alone.

It is conditions such as I have been describing that make the promises of communism seem attractive. The Communist Party has been outlawed and has gone underground throughout this area, but though its actual numbers are small it is a well-trained active group. Its propaganda has played a considerable part in awakening the people of the Middle East to a realization of the miserableness of their lot. And anyone who visits here even briefly can have no doubt that these people are stirring. They are restless and dissatisfied with things as they are—as indeed they should be—and out of their growing political consciousness are beginning to express their dissatisfaction.

I recall so vividly a Syrian working man—a tile worker— to whom I talked in Damascus. Accompanied by a young woman in our legation, who had been doing social work, I walked down a little street, too narrow to permit the passage of a car, and through a door in a blank wall entered a courtyard where tiles were piled high. In the center was a fountain and carved figurines and small trees. From this courtyard we went through another and on into the first room of the little dwelling. This room was reserved for visitors. A little iron stove stood in the middle; a sofa and some chairs were arranged around the walls, and in one corner there was a fine bed with embroidered covers. I was told privately that this bed was probably never used. There were also two small shy children who stared at us out of large black eyes as if we were unfamiliar animals.

I was curious to see the rest of the house, so our host led us through a little outside passageway into another room which, like the first, opened onto the court. Here the furniture was arranged exactly the same way, but the bed was not so elaborate and the room also contained a narrow child's bed. Beyond this apparently was a kitchen, and through a grille in the wall I caught sight of a woman's face and eyes peering curiously at the strange bold creatures with uncovered faces who were so lost to all sense of modesty that they would dare to talk to men who were not their husbands or members of their immediate family.

Back in the visitors' room again we asked our host about wages and working conditions, and he was eloquent in his reply. It was hard for a man to get along; he himself could not earn enough making tiles to support his family. To bring in a little more, he had taken on an additional job— dyeing tiles—but even so it was not enough, not with the price of food and other essential items so high. He was resentful and dissatisfied, and articulate in stating his conviction that something was wrong with conditions when it was impossible for a man to take care of his family, no matter how hard and long he worked.

In spite of his poverty, however, he insisted on making coffee for us before we went; and as I had been told Arab hospitality must never be refused, I accepted. It was, as I had anticipated, very hot, very black.

To digress for a moment, I had soon found out that whomever one visits out there, whether a Bedouin tribesman, a government official, a university professor, or a farmer, one is always served coffee. The traditional Arab coffee, served in tiny half cups, is black and bitter. I do not really care for it very much, but of course I always drank it. To my discomfiture, however, I found that as soon as I returned my cup to the tray it was invariably refilled. I was in a considerable quandary until a kind friend took pity on me and told me that the trick was to give your cup a little shake as you returned it to the tray. This signalled that you had had enough. Thereafter I shook pointedly.

One evening, dining with our Minister to Lebanon, Harold Minor, and his wife, I had an opportunity to see Arab coffee brewed in the traditional way. Earlier in the evening I had thoroughly enjoyed an exhibition of really beautiful native costumes, borrowed for the purpose from a museum in Jerusalem and modeled by some charming young Lebanese women. After dinner the Minors' cook appeared in the entrance to the living room with his coffee-making paraphernalia. First he measured out the coffee beans and then ground them, singing a strange little tune all the while. Precisely at the right moment he added the water. Finally when the bitter brew was ready, it was passed around in the tiniest of cups from which fortunately one is expected to take only a few swallows. It is quite a ceremony and, I realized as I watched, one that requires considerable skill and energy. While the coffee making was going on someone passed around a hubble-bubble pipe, and I thought of the hookah smoked by the caterpillar in *Alice*. It has a long flexible tube and the smoke is cooled and filtered by being drawn through a container of water to which the tube and pipe bowl are attached. All the men tried it, and some of the ladies, but apparently this also demands skill, for, as I remember, only one person was good at it.

To get back to my Damascan tile maker, there is no doubt that he voiced the feelings of the great masses of people in this part of the world. They simply are no longer willing to suffer the grinding poverty and exploitation—whether under their own governments or a foreign power—that they have experienced in the past.

To be fair, the best of the government officials and the responsible businessmen are aware of this growing unrest. In Lebanon I had a delightful and rewarding evening with the President of the Republic, Bechara el Khoury* and his

* Deposed by a military coup, September, 1952

[13]

charming wife, and found them not only keenly conscious of the political and economic situation but eager to talk about possible developments and ways in which our countries could co-operate. Another evening I was entertained at dinner by a wealthy Lebanese businessman, Henri Pharaon, whose home is literally a museum of fabulous art treasures. There, among the group of government officials and businessmen he had invited as my fellow guests, I heard a lively, informed and thoughtful discussion of the problems Lebanon faces. I left convinced that among the people at the top, at least, there were men with the ability, training and enterprise to make good use of any technical and economic help the United States or the United Nations could give.

In Syria and in Jordan, too, I found at the top an awareness of the need for economic development; the businessmen I talked to seemed to recognize that changes were inevitable and that the living conditions of the people must be improved. Factory owners, for example, spoke of the need for better housing for the workers and of their desire to start some kind of housing plans. At the textile mill I inspected in Damascus I was shown with pride the living quarters they had begun to provide for their foremen, and told that as conditions permitted they intended to start a housing project for the rest of their workers. But it was evident—and this was true in Lebanon, too—that it was being done on a charitable or benevolent basis, a kind of paternalism, rather than for sound economic reasons. It was this attitude as much as anything that made me feel that, in Syria and Jordan especially, though they have accepted the thought of change, they have no idea of the number and extent of the changes that will be necessary.

Apparently it is very hard for the ruling classes in these countries to realize that the people's whole conception of their individual rights is changing, and eventually will require a semi-revolution—even to the sharing of profits—before their desire for greater economic rewards and a greater participation in the government can be satisfied.

Neither did it seem to me that they were making the intelligent long-range plans that must precede any real and effective economic development. Here, as in most of the other countries of the Middle East, administrative inefficiency is a real handicap; so is the lack of knowledge of how to meet the diverse problems of organization; so is the lack of trained personnel to carry out the plans after they are made. Of course they have, as I have said, a few trained and energetic people at the top. But to carry out any big long-range improvement, whether in industry, agriculture or government, requires innumerable devoted, well-trained workers—and these people as yet are simply not available. This is such a basic requirement that almost the first thing needed is a system of schools where young people can be educated in various necessary capacities. The experience of other countries, foreign technical experts, teachers, exchange student arrangements and so on could all be very helpful here; but before this is possible Syria and Jordan must first recognize their needs and want co-operation where they can get it. Unfortunately their long experience with the workings of imperialism have made them reluctant to accept, much less to ask for, any help from the big powers.

There is one other circumstance, I am afraid, which those behind any genuine economic or political reform program have to struggle against. The standard of government in all these countries allows for greater self-interest on the part of their public servants than is good for the country. As far as I could see, people—for the most part—do not go into government work unselfishly, with the idea of serving the country and their people; on the contrary, most of them feel it is entirely legitimate to use a government position for private profit. Although this practice is certainly not unknown in our own country, it is not with us an accepted conception of government service, but rather a matter for investigation and prosecution. Obviously, in any country where the point of view of self-interest prevails, the enlightened leaders are going to have an uphill job in instituting permanent and far-reaching reforms. Here again they can be helped by a firm, informed and consistent policy on the part of the United States.

As I traveled about I grew increasingly conscious that the weight of the past lies on all these Arab lands. This is, I think, one reason why they do not move more easily into the present. They think back to the days when, under the banner of Islam, the Arab armies conquered most of the known world; to the days under the Empire when Arab universities and the courts at Baghdad and Damascus were great centers of learning; when as philosophers, poets, mathematicians, astronomers, chemists, they made contributions to science and literature that enriched and influenced the entire world. It is easier for them now to look back upon these conquests and glories of the past than it is to face the problems of today.

In all that I have written, I have been trying to show how many factors one must take into consideration in trying to get at the root reasons for the appalling poverty of the Near and Middle East, how many problems must be tackled —and seemingly all at once. I have not begun to exhaust the list of causes, but I have mentioned enough I think to show the complexity of the situation and the urgency of the need for help.

It is therefore heartening to find that some headway is being made. In February of last year, for instance, Jordan and the United States signed a Point Four agreement under which we contributed over two and a half million dollars and Jordan one million. The money is to be used in various ways but mainly to develop the country's water resources and to set up certain agricultural projects.

Although Syria refused Point Four aid, she has recognized the ferment among the people in various practical ways.

Significant, I think, is the provision in the new constitution adopted in 1950 pointing toward the breaking up of large land holdings, one of the blights on the Arab world. This provision states that "a maximum limit for land ownership shall be prescribed by law." In addition to agricultural colleges in Selenie and Bekaa, and an engineering college in Aleppo, Syria has a fine modern government agricultural experiment station and school some distance outside Damascus. I thought, as I went through it, that in many respects it might have come straight from the United States. There were good people at its head; valuable soil testing and other experiments were being carried out; and excellent courses in animal husbandry, modern agricultural methods and so on were being given. There were seventy-five students in the school, carefully chosen from villages in the surrounding countryside. The idea, of course, was that when they had completed their studies they would return to their villages, to put into practice and to teach others what they had learned. But as nearly as I could tell from the answers to my questions, no plans existed for reaching any large number of villages in a systematic way; or for keeping up and spreading the results of the work through some central control. The people at the school told me that the farmers round about frequently came in for advice and information and really made use of what they learned. Knowing how slow farmers everywhere are to change their ways, I felt privately that until the teaching and example of the school's graduates in their own communities had had a chance to take effect, there would be no very startling improvements.

Lebanon, as contrasted to Syria, has a flourishing Point Four program. Citrus fruits are Lebanon's main export, and new ways to harvest and market them are being developed; hybrid corn is being imported, and there is a project under way to improve the livestock of the country. In the public health field, efforts are being made to stamp out malaria and improve the sanitation of the villages. There are also courses for public health nurses.

Money and technical assistance are also being put into irrigating and electrifying some of the villages. There is a big project of this sort in southern Lebanon, which is very dry. Water supplies are being improved. Students are being sent to the United States to study in our universities.

Incidentally one of the most far-reaching and positive influences in the Middle East today is the American University at Beirut. Almost since the year of its founding in 1866 it has been an integral part of the life of the area. It is here that many of the men in public life in the Near and Middle East received their education, and many others as well who have been successful elsewhere. One of the most beautiful of its fifty or more buildings was given to the University by a businessman in Rio de Janiero in memory of his father, who had been a student there. A nonsectarian institution, it was founded through private donations,

largely American, and is still financed by individual sub-
scriptions and student fees. Under Dr. S. B. L. Penrose, the
present president, it has expanded until it now numbers
some twenty-seven hundred students—both men and
women—of forty different nationalities. It has a medical
school, schools of nursing and pharmacy, a hospital and
several active clinics, which last year served about forty
thousand patients. The students of the medical school do
public health work in the slums and work as interns in the
villages. The University also includes a preparatory school,
a school of arts and sciences, a school of commerce. A new
school of agriculture and an experimental farm, toward
which the Ford Foundation last year contributed half a
million dollars, will further extend and intensify the work
and influence of the University in the entire Arab world.

In addition, the University offers 175 Technical Coopera-
tion Administration fellowships in such subjects as public
health, engineering, industrial chemistry and economics.
These were made possible by a Point Four grant, the fellow-
ship students being selected by the governments of Lebanon, Syria, Jordan and the other Arab countries.
Altogether I found in Lebanon a most encouraging demonstration of what Point Four aid can mean when it is intelligently directed and applied.

Another hopeful sign in the Middle Eastern picture—
one I found particularly encouraging—is the beginning of a
developing social conscience among the Moslem women.

For centuries they have held an inferior position in the
Moslem world and have had almost no rights of any kind.
Wives owed complete obedience to their husbands, who
could divorce them at will—or beat them for impropriety.
They could not appear unveiled in public or participate in
any social activity, even in their own homes, at which men
outside their own families were present. They were not
deemed worthy of an education, and it goes without saying
that they could not vote.

Now, however, the picture is changing—at least to some
extent. Women, particularly among the professional classes,
are beginning to shake off their seclusion, to interest themselves in problems outside their homes. It is not happening
in the Arab countries so rapidly as and to the degree that
it is in Pakistan and India, for there has not been the same
encouragement or incentive. But it is worth noting that
under the new Syrian Constitution women now have the
vote, and some—though not many as yet—are using it.

This trend, if it continues—and I feel sure that it must—
will play an increasingly important part in the awakening
of the peoples of the Near and Middle East and in hasten-
ing the practical measures that will rid them of their grinding poverty.

The Mohammedan religion is felt as a factor not only
in the lives of Moslem women, but in every aspect of Moslem life—social, economic, political. It is a tie that unites
all Moslems everywhere, regardless of country, race or color,

in a kind of religious brotherhood. The trouble is that not only does it unite Moslem and Moslem, but it unites them, in any difference of opinion, against all non-Moslems. Anyone who has not had to reckon with it would find it hard to believe how completely this sense of religious community governs their every act—even at times when self-interest might seem to demand a different course. We have seen how it works politically in the United Nations—for example, in the dispute between France and Tunisia and Morocco. The Arab countries in the Near and Middle East are not really affected by conditions in these French protectorates, yet solely because of the religious tie they are solidly behind the Tunisian and Moroccan demands on France.

We shall see presently how it is working—and to their own detriment—in the case of the Israeli-Arab dispute and how it is affecting the arrangement of a final peace settlement.

Leaving the council halls aside for the moment, their religion reaches even into the kitchen of a Moslem home and controls what they shall eat and how they shall cook it. Certain foods are forbidden; certain foods are permitted, and every Moslem housewife in every Moslem country the world over must follow the same rules in preparing the dishes for her family's meals. There are no local variations.

Considering the preponderance of Moslems in this area, and the dominant role their religion plays in their lives, it is not surprising that religious toleration has not been one of the outstanding characteristics of these countries. An exception is Lebanon. I was glad this country was my introduction to the Middle East, for its policy of religious and political tolerance creates a climate which is more congenial to the Westerner than that he is apt to find in some of the other Arab countries. I, at least, found Lebanon easier to understand. The victims of political upsets or religious wars and persecutions in neighboring states have long found asylum here. The country is also unique in the Middle East in that here Christians outnumber Moslems 55 per cent to 45 per cent. Syria's 3½ million people are largely Moslem, and in Jordan only 90,000 out of some 1½ million are non-Moslems. In the Lebanon Parliament, or Chamber of Deputies as it is called, every religion is represented. The country is divided into religious districts—Moslem, Druse, Christian and so forth—and the delegate elected from each district must be of a corresponding faith.

This does not mean, however, that the Moslems of Lebanon are not as deeply conscious of the Islamic tie as the Moslems anywhere else. There, as in other Arab lands, one is aware always of the religion of Mohammed as a pervasive, sometimes subtle, but powerful force. This may not be an altogether happy situation for us, any more than it is, in my opinion, for them. Nevertheless, we had better be aware of it and watch it. For just as the Soviet Union has made a religion out of a political creed—communism—so, by a kind of reverse twist, the followers of Islam have made their religion an integral and controlling part of their political life.

The problem that seems to me to overshadow every other in the entire Middle East is the fate of the Arab refugees from Palestine. This is what everyone was most eager to talk to me about. The feeling behind the original opposition of the Arab states to the creation of Israel as an independent nation was, of course, only intensified when in the late spring of 1948 the new Zionist state was actually proclaimed. The opposition of the Arabs, conflicting with the determination of the Jews to hold what they felt was rightfully theirs, resulted inevitably in open warfare. At the end of the fighting, Israel was in possession not only of the territory designated as hers by the United Nations, but half again as much, including the New City part of Jerusalem, though the Arabs still held the Old City. When the United Nations reaffirmed its decision to internationalize Jerusalem, it got no support from either side, and the fighting continued until February, 1949, when, through the efforts of Dr. Ralph Bunche, the UN mediator, an armistice was signed. About ten months later, in December, 1949, Israel announced she was moving her capital to Jerusalem.

Hapless victims of the conflict were approximately 800,-000 Arabs living in Palestine, who during the fighting fled to neighboring Arab countries. Most of them are now living in refugee camps, unassimilated and unwanted either by the country of refuge or by Israel. They simply exist—

wretchedly, hopelessly, a constant thorn in the side of the Arab body politic, and a continuing source of bitter controversy between Israel and the Arab states.

What makes it difficult for the visitor who goes there, as I did, with a desire to get a rounded, balanced picture of the situation is that on this subject everyone's thinking is completely colored by his emotions. All one can do is to get the Arab point of view in the Arab countries, the Israeli point of view in Israel, balance them against each other and against one's own background of information.

For example, during one of my early press conferences, when questioned on my interpretation of the Balfour Declaration, I said I had always assumed that when Lord Balfour pledged British support for a Jewish national home in Palestine, he had meant that the Jews should have their own country under their own government. I was told that not only did the Declaration not mean this, but that Lord Balfour had told the Jewish leader, Chaim Weizmann, that it did not. I recalled a conversation I had once had with Dr. Weizmann at Lake Success, in which he told me what Lord Balfour had said to him. Since his account accorded with my own understanding, and both were so completely at variance with the interpretation now advanced by my Arab questioners, I decided this was simply one of those emotional questions about which feelings run so high that neither side can concede even the possibility of another point of view.

But I also determined that while I was in the Arab countries I was going to get as clear a picture as possible in my mind of the way they saw the question. For this I found one cannot do better than to talk to the professors at the American University at Beirut. They give one an excellent account of the Arab side of any controversy between the Arab nations and Israel. At a tea given for me by Dr. Penrose and his wife, a number of us sat around in a circle and talked for a long time. They feel very strongly that the crux of the trouble was the partition of Palestine and the creation of Israel as an independent state; this they are convinced was a serious mistake on the part of the United Nations, along with our earlier encouragement of the Jews' desire for independence. What the Arabs had urged was independence for Palestine as a whole, with the Jews to be a protected minority. They contend that during the years when Palestine was governed as an entity under the British mandate, there had been no trouble between Arabs and Jews; they had lived together there side by side, peacefully and harmoniously. Trouble started only when the Jews began trying to set up a separate government of their own. Remembering the Arab-Jewish riots in Jerusalem in 1929, one may question the soundness of this argument. Nevertheless, that is the way the Arabs feel, deeply and sincerely. They also feel that we are continuing to favor Israel at their expense. Some of the people in responsible positions there, including Dr. Penrose, warn us that if this thought becomes fixed and widespread enough, the peoples of the Arab nations may well turn for help toward Moscow.

So there is bitterness and resentment; and there is also fear. Israel has received something like 700,000 immigrants in the last few years both from Europe and from neighboring Arab states. Observing this constant stream of immigration, the Arabs are haunted by the fear that Israel will soon become too crowded and will then try to expand by taking over more Arab territory. I tried to make them understand that their surest defense was in a strong United Nations that opposed aggression everywhere; but I am afraid that I was not successful in allaying their fear.

Paradoxically, they will sometimes tell you that the Arabs have long memories and someday will drive the people of Israel into the sea—a claim not altogether consistent with their expressed fear of Israeli aggression. However, I discovered long ago that people are seldom consistent when faced with a difficult and emotional situation.

Bitter though the responsible officials are, they can—quite understandably—talk more objectively about the Arab-Israeli difficulties than can the refugees themselves.

While I was in Beirut a group of educated refugees invited me to visit them and hear their stories. They told me how cruelly they had been driven from their homes in Palestine and forced to abandon their possessions at a moment's notice. Though these particular people were among the few fortunate ones who have found an opportunity to practice their professions and build a new life, their eviction still rankled and they declared they would never be satisfied until they could return to their homes in Palestine.

I liked these people and felt desperately sorry for them, realizing that they are simply the helpless victims of the history of their times, and have been caught in a struggle that is beyond their understanding. But though I sympathized with them, my greatest sympathy went to the vast majority who have not been able to find work and who are still living in refugee camps.

Conditions in the camps I visited are pitiful. In some of them only a few hundred may be quartered, in others as many as sixteen thousand may be living in tents pitched on steep hillsides or set up on hot, barren plains where the dust swirls constantly. In one hillside camp I saw, many of the tents had been blown down the night before in a storm. Scorpions and poisonous snakes are a constant menace. One distraught mother led me to the spot where a snake had bitten her baby only a few hours ago. Happily prompt treatment had saved its life.

Other refugees—perhaps more fortunate—are housed in mosques. Here, for each family one little square partitioned off by sacking is "home." In a corner a small one-burner primus stove serves for all the cooking that is done.

In all the camps respiratory diseases take a big toll in the winter, dysentery and fevers in summer. Undernourished and dispirited people do not have much resistance. There are hospitals of course, where doctors and nurses give the best care they can, but the situation is not very satisfactory.

I could not find much consolation in the fact that most of the people came originally from homes that were none too comfortable in any case and so were used to poor living. For the others—and there are a number of them, I am told—who were professional people in comfortable circumstances, living under the conditions in these camps must be intolerable.

All these refugees, except for the small minority who have managed to make new lives for themselves outside the camps, have been for the past four years under the care of the United Nations Relief and Works Agency for Palestine Refugees. And their number is constantly being increased by the infiltration of Arabs from the desert, where food is even scarcer than it is in the camps. What food, what clothing, what shelter, what medical care, what education these people have had has been provided through the United Nations Agency, though the Red Cross has helped out where it could. But very little has been done for them by the countries of their asylum. Jordan, to be sure, has taken steps toward absorbing into its economy some of the approximately 600,000 refugees within its borders. It has granted them citizenship and permits them to leave the camps and find work—if they can. And there is some hope that its UN-backed 50-million-dollar irrigation program may eventually give work to 150,000 of them. But Jordan, with its large nomad population and agricultural economy, has a serious unemployment problem without the addition of refugees, and opportunities are limited. Certainly the small efforts that have been made toward their resettlement have not been on any scale commensurate with the problem. Syria has plenty of land and needs settlers, but it has not granted its refugees citizenship, nor made any real attempt to use them. In Lebanon the refugees are perhaps in the worst case of all. Again it is partly an economic problem, since the country cannot now feed or provide employment for its own citizens, let alone a flood of refugees. But there is also the fact that, as I have explained, representation in the Lebanon Parliament is based on religious rather than political groups, and no one wants to see the present delicate balance upset, as it would be by the permanent addition to the population of some 100,000 refugees. This is perfectly understandable; nevertheless, the fact remains that while Lebanon will accept refugees on a temporary basis as long as the UN will support them, it will do nothing to encourage them to feel they are permanently settled. Consequently, the refugees in the Lebanese camps think of their situation as a temporary one and make no effort to find work or to occupy themselves constructively in the camps. For after all, will they not soon be going home?

The tragedy is not only that as things stand they are an economic burden on the country that harbors them, a fertile field for Communist agitators and a storehouse of dynamite as far as the peace of the Middle East is concerned. The greater tragedy to my mind is the loss of skills, the death of pride, the breakdown of morale—in short, the human waste and the deterioration that is the inevitable result of enforced idleness and a seemingly hopeless future. In all my talks with Arab officials and others in responsible positions, I protested that these people, whether in the end they were to be repatriated or resettled, would be of no future use unless their skills and work habits were preserved. And unless the older ones passed on what they knew to the younger ones, none of them would be of any use ever, anywhere. My arguments always met with at least passive agreement, but it was an agreement born, I felt, of perfect politeness—and complete inertia.

So they go on, nearly 800,000 refugees, figuratively and literally rotting away, depending on the UN for every basic need, living only for the day they can return to the homes they were forced to leave. In many cases, I am sure, these homes have long since been destroyed, but that is a possibility no one would dare suggest to any of them.

I could not help wondering whether in all instances this precipitate flight from Palestine was absolutely necessary. Of course, as in all wars, atrocities were perpetrated by both sides, and certainly the Arabs were told stories and shown pictures of cruelties committed during the fighting between Israeli and Arab forces. In one case the entire population of a Moslem town was massacred one night; and I was told during a United Nations meeting of another place where innocent people were killed and thrown down a well, their bodies later to be recovered by the Red Cross.

One cannot be surprised that such things happened, nor can one blame the people that fled, for they were obviously driven by a great fear; also there is no doubt that they expected to return shortly with the victorious Arab armies. But one is surprised that they would leave places that were fairly safe, unless from panic and hysteria spread through authoritative channels. And it is a fact that some of the villages that were evacuated were not threatened at all or even in the path of the fighting. It is also a fact that some 170,000 Moslems are still living peacefully and unharmed in Israel. The truth is that the Arab authorities are to a large extent responsible for this wholesale flight. Mass evacuation was apparently a part of their strategy. They urged the people to leave, assuring them of the quick success of the Arab armies. Then, they were promised, not only would they get back their own land but would share in the spoils won from the Israelis. Arab responsibility for the present situation must be shared, it seeems to me, by the British, who furnished the refugees with transportation.

But memories are short when people suffer, and today most of the people in the camps, thinking only of what they have lost, put the blame for their wretched plight on Israel and the United States rather than on their own leaders and the British.

Meanwhile the Arab leaders find it to their interest to keep alive the bitter feeling, using as a political weapon the demands of an unhappy people to have their wrongs righted.

All attempts by the United Nations to settle the differences between Arabs and Israelis have been balked by the intransigence of both sides. The Arabs insist that Israel must repatriate or compensate all refugees; to this Israel will not —and indeed cannot—agree. But so long as both sides continue to pin full responsibility for the refugee problem on the other, they will never be able to come to terms on the ultimate disposition of the refugees. And until they do, the hostility between them will remain a menace to the peace and stability of the entire Middle East.

The sooner this ominous fact is faced, the better it will be for all. The past must be forgotten and the future must be made possible by the international community. The United Nations, to be sure, is doing what it can; last year it made available 2½ million dollars for rehabilitation projects and the director of its Arab Refugee Agency reported that some headway had been made in improving living conditions in the camps. But all this is no final solution. Prejudices and feelings must be put aside and the whole refugee problem looked upon as an economic one. Israel must realize the benefit to her of establishing peaceful relations. She needs the resources of the Arab countries; she needs Arab oil, and food and raw materials. A final peace settlement would make all these available to her, and available in even greater measure if she could send her trained administrators and skilled technicians to help the Arabs modernize their methods and develop their so far untapped resources.

Obviously the Arabs too would gain immeasurably if such friendly arrangements were possible. The industry and energy of the Jews of Israel, the skills, the organizing ability and technical knowledge they brought with them from other countries, if applied to some of the problems of the Arab economy, could do much to raise the standard of living in every country in this area. But the Arab League has forbidden its members to have relations of any kind with Israel; they cannot even import the products Israel manufactures which they need.

Instead the Arabs still talk hopefully of wiping out the people of Israel. I have a feeling that this would not be easy. Even if it were possible, such a war would be a grievous thing. The immediate suffering it would cause is obvious. But I am thinking also of the fact that although the Arabs would gain some land, perhaps, and the refugees could return to what homes they have left, they would not put into the country the hard and intelligent work that the Jews have. And unless they did, all development would stop; the land would deteriorate, barren plains and dry deserts would appear where tree-planted fields and productive farms now flourish. The loss would be not only to the people of Israel, but to the future development of the entire Middle East.

2

Israel: A Dedicated Land

All along the way as we drove from Amman, in Jordan, to Jerusalem I began to feel the reality of the Bible story. The road leads over the Moab Mountains to Jericho past the place where John the Baptist baptized Christ in the Jordan, and on to the Dead Sea, on whose barren and desolate shores Lot's wife was turned into a pillar of salt. From Jericho the road winds upward almost four thousand feet to Jerusalem, atop Judea.

Wandering about Jerusalem, I came to realize vividly how truly it is the holy city of three great faiths—Christian, Hebrew and Moslem. One place seemed to me particularly to symbolize this thought. In the Arab section of the city stands the first really beautiful mosque I had seen—the Mosque of Omar, or more properly, the Dome of the Rock. It is built on the site of Solomon's Temple, which was destroyed by the Babylonians under Nebuchadnezzar, and one section of its western wall is the Wailing Wall of the Jews. Inside the mosque under its huge round dome is the rock where Abraham is said to have taken Isaac to sacrifice. To the Moslems it is the Rock of the Ascension, the rock from which Mohammed is supposed to have made his night journey to heaven. Next to Mecca, it is their most sacred shrine.

Then we walked along the Via Dolorosa, the crooked narrow street through which Jesus is thought to have passed on his way to Calvary. Plaques let into the walls of the buildings mark the various stations of the Cross, the places where he is said to have stumbled or rested, and at the end of the Way is the Church of the Holy Sepulchre, built on the supposed site of Jesus' tomb.

Everywhere I went in the Old City, I was deeply conscious of the hundreds and hundreds of years that had passed, and I had a curious feeling that neither the people nor the streets had changed much since the days of Christ. Then abruptly I would be reminded of the present, and of the Holy Land's stalemated war. There were, for instance, the unused buildings of the Hebrew University and of the Rothschild-Hadassah Medical Center on Mount Scopus. The University was formally opened in 1925, and for about a quarter of a century expanded rapidly. However, during the fighting that broke out in Jerusalem between the Jews and the Arabs even before the partition of Palestine went into effect, the Jewish community there, cut off from Israel, was forced to surrender in the Old City, though they managed to hold out in the New City until Israeli relief forces arrived. After the armistice was signed, the Old City, along with the other areas in Palestine held by the Arab Legion at the conclusion of the fighting, was annexed by Jordan. Unfortunately the University on Mount Scopus is in the Old City part of Jerusalem, so the Jews are now denied access to their great center of learning.

Another reminder of the physical division of Jerusalem came when, after attending a memorial service for King George VI, we prepared to cross over into the New City. For the Arab side and the Jewish side are separated by a guarded barrier which stretches clear across the road. We drove up to it promptly at noon, passage through having been arranged before I left Paris. At exactly the minute agreed upon the barrier was raised. Alighting from our car, we walked through accompanied by Mr. Tyler, the American consul, who, though he lives on the Jewish side of Jerusalem, is permitted to go back and forth.

To cross from the Arab lands into Israel was in one striking way a curious experience. Though one was still in a country where many of the people were by religion Moslems, Christians or Druses, the population was of course predominantly Jewish. Naturally this fact is reflected in the make-up of the government, in the educational system and in many other ways—for instance, one cannot easily get a taxi on Saturday; nevertheless I had no feeling here that religion was the controlling factor it was in the Arab countries I had visited. Israel is a secular state, a democracy. Most of its people have come from countries of the Western world, and I felt more at home there, closer to the modern life and Western attitudes I was familiar with, than in any other country I visited.

These people are not daunted by Arab threats. Being Jews, they have been spurned and persecuted in every country on earth, and they have learned to fight for their very existence. Now that at last they have a small piece of land of their own, it does not frighten them that they may be called upon to defend it.

And it is a very small piece of land, in area even smaller than the state of New Jersey. Pressed up against the Mediterranean, hemmed in on the north, east and south by Moslem countries, it is about 260 miles long, about 5 miles wide at its narrowest point, about 70 at its widest. Only the narrow coastal plain is well watered and fertile. In the semi-desert of the Negev, the southern triangle of Israel, agriculture is difficult. Irrigation projects, drawing on the waters of the Jordan, are gradually opening the northern Negev to cultivation, but in the south only dry farming methods are possible. Only by the most consecrated effort, the utilization of every modern technique and a willingness to experiment, can Israel support her own growing population, which now amounts to some 1½ million. By no stretch of the imagination, for this reason if for no other, can I envisage the return of the 800,000 destitute refugees now in Arab lands.

Nevertheless, the government has made an effort to treat

fairly the Moslems who remained in Israel. In the Proclamation of the State of Israel in 1948, they were bidden to "play their part in the development of the State on the basis of full and equal citizenship." There is an Arab party which is represented in the Knesset (the Israeli parliament); there are public schools for Arabs as well as Hebrews, and schooling is compulsory. There is, of course, freedom of worship. It is true, however, that the Israeli Nationality Bill, passed shortly after I was there, confers automatic citizenship on Jews only; most of the Arabs will have to go through a lengthy naturalization process to achieve this status.

I spent six days in Israel where, as we had arranged, Miss Corr and I were joined by Dr. David Gurewitsch. They were days in which every minute was packed with activity. This country teems with life and purpose. Everyone seems to be engaged in one kind of project or another—reforesting the hillsides, draining the swamps, irrigating the land, restoring its topsoil, building towns and roads, starting new industries, training newly arrived immigrants. Under the guidance of Mr. Michael Comay, an able and charming young man from the Foreign Office, who had come to Israel from South Africa, and his indefatigable assistant, Mr. Gideon, who accompanied us everywhere, we were shown a good number of the remarkable things that were being done. Dr. Chaim Sheba, a delightful man and dedicated public servant, who is establishing a health service throughout Israel, was also with us on several trips.

Particularly interesting to me always were the difficulties that had been overcome. In northeast Israel, for example, there is a lake named Bahr-el-Huleh, through which flow the headwaters of the River Jordan. In draining the Huleh swamps it was necessary to change the course of the river. But no dirt from the river bed could be thrown up on its eastern shore—for that was Arab territory. In one place, a few small parcels of Arab-owned land meant that instead of cutting a straight channel for the flow of the river, it was necessary to dredge a wide curve. All operations had to be carried on from the Israeli side—but it was done. When I asked the engineer if it hadn't been a frustrating experience, his answer was, "Without difficulties, it would have been no fun."

This was a point of view I found cropping up everywhere. One of the factories I visited made pipe which was used to carry water from the Jordan into the semiwasteland of the Negev. The foreman of the plant is a redheaded young New Englander, who has under him Jews with varying religious customs, including a number of Yemenites. The kingdom of Yemen is a little country south of Saudi Arabia on the Red Sea coast. The Jews who came from there are particularly orthodox. For centuries they lived in the same way, keeping apart from the rest of the population, clinging to their old customs. They could not speak Hebrew when they started arriving in Israel a few decades ago, and their only tie with the other Jews there was their religion.

This particular group, though skilled with their hands, had never worked in a factory before, and for a while they had a number of industrial accidents. One morning, the young foreman told me, several of them waited upon him and said, "These accidents occur because the Lord is displeased with us. We must make a sacrifice to the Lord at the plant."

He did not wish to dampen their ardor, but meat supplies are scarce in Israel, and in order to sacrifice a sheep, as they desired, they would first have to get permission from the food administrator to buy one. He helped them draft the necessary letter, and in time an answer came back, denying their request. In the meantime, however, the Yemenites had been learning rapidly and accidents had become rare. Therefore, when he imparted the sad news that no sheep would be available, they answered, "The Lord must have been satisfied with our intentions. He has already relieved us of the burden of His displeasure."

All this must have seemed strange to a young Yankee foreman, but he apparently has been infected by the enthusiasm of everyone around him. The problems of training and dealing with these people are to him simply part of his job, a challenge that lends it spice. Pipes have to be made; they have to be laid, and water must run through them. No matter what the difficulties are, this is going to be done.

The growing town of Beersheba at the head of the Negev

affords another demonstration of how untrained immigrants are gradually integrated into the Israeli life and economy. The mayor of the town was originally a Czech, with a passion for building and an intuitive knowledge of how to help people develop their abilities.

During their first year, the immigrants live in one-room shacks and are put to work on the simplest kind of construction. By the second year they have learned to use many strange and complicated tools that they had never seen in the country from which they came—perhaps Morocco, or Iran, or Yemen. They then move into a two-room house with a garden, and are given work on bigger and more elaborate buildings. The third year they are ready to live wherever they want to, and with the skills they have acquired can be given employment on large two- and three-storied apartment houses.

Along with the housing construction, sites for new industries are being prepared. As the city expands, the industries will move in and absorb the labor now engaged in building. Under the wise direction of the mayor, Beersheba will in time become a modern, well-planned city.

Israel is determined to industrialize and is pushing its program rapidly. At present its industries are for the most part on a small scale, but it does have a great variety of the so-called light manufactures—especially processed foods, textiles, clothing and so on, both for export and for home consumption. However, the government has wisely encouraged foreign investment by low tax rates and by permitting the withdrawal abroad of a large percentage of the profits. Consequently, there has been a considerable flow of capital equipment for large industrial enterprises. Most of this activity is concentrated in and around Haifa, where Israel also has an important oil refinery. I visited a large Kaiser-Frazer plant there which is operating almost entirely for export to Scandinavia. The Alliance Tire and Rubber Company, I am told, has opened a pilot plant in Hadera, and I believe a number of other big American firms have made good-sized investments.

Despite all its industrial expansion, Israel's economic mainstay is still agriculture. Here, on the farms, in the orchards and vineyards, people go at their tasks with the same crusading zeal and imagination I found everywhere. I was particularly interested in visiting Degania, one of the older communal agricultural settlements, where I spent the night. The land in this village was bought originally by the Israel Development Corporation, a Zionist group. All land, all property, is owned in common. The people live together, eat together in a common dining room. The community provides a school, and a nursery where the babies and young children are cared for during the day while their mothers are at work. No one receives any money for his work; indeed he has no need of money, for the community supplies him with everything from pins and toothpaste to clothes, food and medical care. If money should be

[43]

needed for a trip or vacation, the community supplies that too.

This particular village had an extremely interesting natural history project. The people had built a museum and made a most comprehensive collection of the local flora and fauna, which were now being used in valuable agricultural and scientific studies. The head of the museum had made a special study of the insects of the region and could tell you exactly what species were to be found and where, the season when they were most numerous, even the hours when they were most active. His data had helped greatly in eliminating malaria in this region.

This settlement had played a heroic part in the Arab-Israeli War. The story was told me by Joseph Baratz, a vigorous old man, well over sixty, who is the head of the village. Telling it with great spirit, he seemed to be living through it all over again. When he heard that the Syrian army was moving in their direction, he said, he went to David Ben Gurion, now Prime Minister of Israel, to get aid. The villagers had no arms, of course, since under the British mandate Jews were forbidden to own weapons. There might have been a smuggled gun here and there, but certainly nothing with which they could oppose the Syrian army. Mr. Baratz begged Ben Gurion for soldiers, or at least weapons, but was told there were none available. He was to go back to his people, Ben Gurion said, and to stay with them; let them fight with their agricultural imple-

ments. He went back and told his people they must die defending their homes and their land. They dug a ditch, and
as the Syrian army approached across the plains south of
Lake Tiberias, the villagers prepared to oppose it as a living
wall. If the enemy broke through at this point, there would
be nothing to stop it from sweeping down the totally
unprotected valley.

Standing on the edge of the ditch he had helped to dig
four years before, Mr. Baratz continued with the story so
vividly I felt I could see the army coming. In the lead were
tanks. As the first one reached the very edge of the ditch, an
old man of sixty-odd rose up and threw a Molotov cock-
tail—a crude, homemade bomb—right into the tank. There
was an explosion; the tank stopped; and the army hesitated
and then began to retreat. Israel was saved from invasion at
this point by that one act of heroism. Luck? Perhaps in
part, but also great faith, devotion and courage.

What is left of the tank still stands at the edge of the
ditch, a silent reminder—and a monument.

It is clear that agricultural communities such as this one
are not merely economic projects to these people, but an
entire way of life, of living and working together. They apparently take great hold of the young people who are captured by the communal idea, for though they may leave
for a few years to serve in the army or to try a different
kind of life, they usually return and want to stay. I am told
that they also have a special appeal for older people, for

there is no question they offer complete security. People in their middle years, however, are apt to prefer more independence than the completely communal settlement, or the Kibbutz as it is called, affords.

There are several other types of agricultural communities. One is the co-operative. Here each person owns his own land and lives his own private life, but buys all his necessary equipment—grain, tools, fertilizer or whatever—and sells his produce through a co-operative.

Another kind combines features of both the communal settlement and the co-operative. Here, as I understand it, the villagers own the land in common, and the marketing and purchasing is done by the community as in the Kibbutz. However, each family lives in its own home, and has a small garden for its own use.

A good many of these communities, in addition to their farming, run a small industry on the side—perhaps a creamery or a knitting mill or some kind of handicraft project.

I should add that membership in any of these organizations is purely voluntary. About 60 per cent of the farm population do belong to one or another of them by choice, but the rest operate as independently as any farmer in the United States.

The remarkable thing to me about Israel is its diversity, its elasticity. A new small state, fighting a war for its very life, remaking a land worn out by centuries of misuse, build-

At the home of Ambassador and Mrs. Minor in Beirut. *Above left:* Coffee made in the Arab way. *Right:* Trying the Arab water pipe. *Below:* Visiting refugees at the Dekwani camp.

Above: At the American school outside Beirut. *Below:* At refugee camps in Lebanon the older boys are given vocational training to fit them for the future.

Above: Children at play, and a kindergarten class at camps in Lebanon where refugees live in tents. Below: A fashion show is staged for Mrs. Roosevelt at the home of Ambassador and Mrs. Minor.

Above: Mrs. Roosevelt signs the book at the Presidency in Damascus. With her are Miss Corr, a police officer, the Secretary at the Presidency, and the American Minister. *Left:* She is received by the Secretary, Mr. Abdullah Khani.

Throughout her trip Mrs. Roosevelt met and talked with members of the press.
Here she is shown with a representative group in Amman, Jordan.

Above: The engineer of the project explains to Mrs. Roosevelt the draining of the Huleh swamps at the border of Israel and Jordan. *Below:* Approaching the hospital from Town Hall in Beersheba. With Mrs. Roosevelt are Dr. Mann, Julia Dushkin, and an aide-de-camp, followed by a crowd of citizens.

Above left: Mrs. Roosevelt talking with Sheikh Suleiman and Colonel Michael Hanegbi, Governor of the Beersheba area, who has been working for co-operation between the Arabs and the Jews. *Above right:* A church maintained by the Franciscans in Nazareth. *Below:* Mrs. Roosevelt with her party in the basement of the building, which is said to have been the kitchen of the Virgin Mary.

Above: Arriving in Karachi, Mrs. Roosevelt inspects the guard of honor presented by the Pakistan Women's National Guard. *Below:* Begum Shahabuddin, President of the All-Pakistan Women's Association, North-West Frontier Province, presents Mrs. Roosevelt with a chogha (long coat) and a golden garland.

Above left: Mrs. Roosevelt is introduced to the Maliks of the Tribal Jirgas in the Khyber Pass. *Above right:* She examines the handmade pistol they presented to her. *Below left:* The dopatta Mrs. Roosevelt is wearing was given to her by the Karachi branch of the All-Pakistan Women's Association. *Below right:* A primary school at Quaidabad, Karachi, for refugee children.

Above: Mrs. Roosevelt arrives in New Delhi. *Left to right:* Chester Bowles, Madame Pandit, Mrs. Roosevelt, Major Yunus Khan, Jawaharlal Nehru, Rajkumari Amrit Kaur and Mrs. Bowles. *Left:* Greeting the Burmese Ambassador at a reception given by Prime Minister Nehru in New Delhi. *Below:* Mrs. Roosevelt adopts the Indian gesture of greeting as she is introduced to Jagjivam Ram, Labor Minister, and H. K. Mehta, Minister for Commerce and Industry.

Above: An interested exchange between Mrs. Roosevelt and Dr. K. N. Katju, Finance Minister. *Right:* Mrs. Roosevelt calls on President Prasad. *Below:* Chatting with the Honorable Shri Patanjali Shastri, Chief Justice of India, and Rajkumari Amrit Kaur, Minister of Health.

Above: On a visit to a girls' college, Miranda House, in New Delhi. *Left:* Talking to the Philippine Ambassador to India, at a reception given by President Prasad. *Below:* Mrs. Roosevelt with President Prasad and Ambassador and Mrs. Bowles.

Above: A memorial marks the spot where Mahatma Gandhi was assassinated.
Below: Kandarya Mahadeva Temple, Khajuraha, near New Delhi.

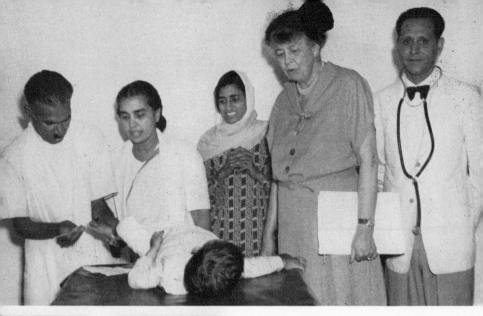

Above: During a visit to the Faridabad Refugee Colony, Mrs. Roosevelt inspects the Abdul Gaffar Khan Hospital and (left) the spinning center. Below: Touring the village of Palli, near New Delhi, to study rural conditions.

Above: A village scene near New Delhi. Right: Mrs. Roosevelt greets an Untouchable woman. Below: At a village well.

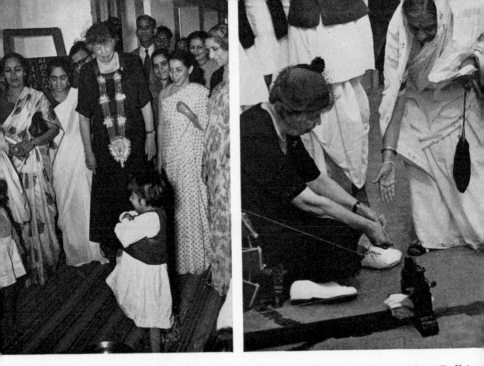

Above left: A visit to the Refugee Women's Colony at Lajpat Nagar, New Delhi. *Above right:* At the Harijan Colony with Rameshwari Nehru, Mrs. Roosevelt is shown how a spinning wheel works. *Below:* Boys of the Harijan Colony working on charkhas.

ing industries where none ever existed, it has at the same time absorbed and resettled hundreds of thousands of immigrants of widely different backgrounds, skills, education and nationalities. To fuse all these it has had to improvise, to experiment, to adapt, to stretch here and tighten there, in order to adjust the people to the country and the country to the needs of the people.

There were even people who could do nothing for themselves. For example, a shipload of blind immigrants arrived from Morocco. For them the government established a special village, where, with the aid of the sighted members of their families, they have been taught skills that enable them to earn their own living. They work in the gardens and in the auxiliary industry, and the products of their labor are sold through a co-operative. The village, which has a blind mayor, is so well organized that these people lead a more nearly normal life than in any institution I have ever seen. Throughout the little settlement there was an atmosphere of harmony and real happiness.

Even more remarkable to me were the children's villages, many of them sponsored by Youth Aliyah. Here lived children who in the past had suffered beyond belief. Many of them had lost every member of their family and had wandered desolate and unwanted for years. Others had come from places like Morocco or other Moslem countries where their living conditions had been nothing short of horrifying. Now they are uniformly secure and happy. They have

[47]

good schools; they are loved and cared for by older people who are training them to look after themselves, to grow their own food and govern their own villages. Out of those pitiful stunted waifs, to raise children who are healthy and strong and imbued with a love for the land and their country—this is perhaps Israel's most extraordinary achievement.

In its few years of statehood, this small republic has faced a desperate financial crisis. In 1951 it applied for Point Four aid, which it is now putting to good use. It also floated a $500 million bond issue, with Ben Gurion traveling to America in its support. The $715 million in reparations that the Bonn government in Germany has agreed to pay will help in its development program and in rehabilitating the victims of Nazi aggression. Grants-in-aid from the U. S. and a loan from the International Bank have also helped. Nevertheless, the country is far from being out of the woods yet. Much hinges on a peaceful solution to the Arab refugee question. When all the great creative ability of Israel can be freed from concern with armaments and defense and directed toward its internal well-being, Arabs as well as Jews will profit, and the world will have in the Middle East its strongest bulwark against communism.

David Ben Gurion, Israel's Prime Minister, is a lion of a man with a heart of gold. Even to his own co-workers he is almost a legendary figure. They will tell you that the man must never sleep. He reads everything; he knows everything; and yet he never seems tired. I do not know the secret of his vitality and strength—whether it is his power of quick recuperation or simply his absorption in his job —but Israel is indeed fortunate to have such a man to pilot it through the troublous early days of its democracy.

This I do know: that in everyone from Ben Gurion down to the most unimportant government official, the least worker on the land or in the factory, I encountered a determination and a sense of dedication that filled me with confidence. So much spirit, so much resolve, cannot possibly be without result; they must, sooner or later, make this experiment a success.

3

As Pakistan Sees It

After our last busy day in Israel we got up before dawn the next morning to take a plane from Lydda to Karachi, the capital of Pakistan. There I was to be the guest of the All Pakistan Women's Association which, with the co-operation of the Pakistan government, had planned and arranged a full and varied schedule for me. The original invitation had been extended to me by the president of the Association, the Begum Liaquat Ali Khan, when she was visiting the United States with her husband, the late Prime Minister of Pakistan, in 1950.

Here as earlier in Israel, and later in India, I saw a country not only struggling with the problems that beset any young government, but also suffering from the results of the partition that had accompanied the achievement of their long-sought independence. Geographically and economically, if not religiously, India and Pakistan are a natural unit, a vast, potentially rich peninsula stretching from the snow- and ice-covered mountains of the Himalayas on the north, southward to the Indian Ocean. The division of this

[50]

subcontinent into two independent states, one predominantly Hindu, the other predominantly Moslem, was
economically painful to both parts. India, for example,
though retaining the majority of physical assets, lost much of
her best farm land. Pakistan had wheat enough and to spare
in good years, and a tremendous jute production—80 per
cent of the world's total—but no jute mills. These were all
on India's side of the partition line. She was producing
about 200,000 tons of cotton a year, but she had few textile
mills. India, on the other hand, where cotton manufacturing
is the biggest industry, became largely dependent upon Pakistan for supplies. Pakistan, indeed, had very few industries
of any kind—no tanneries, no woolen mills, for instance—
almost no coal, very little oil. She had, to be sure, a huge
hydroelectric potential, but it was largely untapped. There
is an extensive irrigation system in Pakistan, where eight out
of every ten people depend on the land for a living, but she
lost to India and Kashmir control of the headwaters of the
rivers that fill her canals. Her only really good port was
Karachi; for Chittagong in East Pakistan had been sub-
jected to intense strain during the war and was badly in
need of repairs.

From the point of view of defense too, the subcontinent
is paying a terrible price for partition. The mountain ranges
guarding its northern border made undivided India a
single defense system. The Khyber Pass was one of the few
breaks through which invasion was possible. However, the

Pass is so narrow and the territory so forbidding that it used to be comparatively easy to defend. But the sword of partition not only divided the land, cutting off crops from markets and factories from raw materials, it also split up everything from debts and revenues to rolling stock and typewriters—including, of course, the army. So today instead of a single, strong, united army deployed to meet possible aggression from without, two lesser separate armies must defend the frontiers of the subcontinent. And, instead of facing outward, these two armies now face each other across a line in Kashmir, over which India and Pakistan are at odds.

The history of this quarrel is too involved to go into in detail here. Briefly, what happened is this: under the plan by which power was transferred from the British Raj to India and Pakistan, most of the 565 princely states of India, which had only a treaty relationship with the British Crown—as distinct from the provinces ruled directly by the British— acceded either to India or to Pakistan. But the Hindu Maharajah of Kashmir delayed making any decision until pushed into it by a large-scale invasion of tribesmen coming mainly from Pakistan's North-West Frontier Province. Then, though more than three-fourths of his people were Moslems, he belatedly acceded to India. Pakistan on various grounds disputed the accession; in December of 1947 at the height of the crisis the quarrel was taken to the United Nations, which so far has not been able to work out a solution acceptable to both sides. Under Dr. Frank P. Graham, the United Nations mediator, both countries have agreed to a plebiscite, but they cannot agree on the conditions under which the plebiscite is to be held. Meanwhile bad feeling has continued to mount as Indian and Pakistani troops face each other across a cease-fire line in Kashmir.

As in the case of the Israeli-Arab dispute, bitterness and fear of one's neighbor—here at least partly engendered by the quarrel over Kashmir—has resulted in spending for defense huge sums badly needed for health, housing, educational and other programs that would better the living standards of the people.

Unhappy though some of the consequences of partition may be, there is no question that by the time the British left India, the strength of the Moslem demand for a separate country of their own had made an independent Pakistan inevitable. In a sense, the rivalry between Hindus and Moslems might be said to date back almost to the eighth century, when the Arabs and Afghans began making small raids into India. In the year 1001, Mahmud of Ghazni, coming out of Afghanistan, crossed the Hindu Kush and filed through the Khyber Pass to lead the first of the great Moslem invasions. Until then, for thousands of years the Hindus had dominated the subcontinent, and had developed a highly advanced civilization and a rich culture; but for seven centuries thereafter, the Moslems remained virtually supreme.

From the twelfth to the sixteenth centuries waves of Moslem invaders continued to sweep in from the west, each carving out a separate little kingdom. In the early sixteenth century a Central Asian prince named Baber, a descendant of Tamerlane and Genghis Khan, founded the great Mogul empire which at its height controlled most of India and lasted until the eighteenth century. Then weakened and torn by incessant Hindu revolts, the empire fell apart, while various European powers made haste to stake out their own claims on the subcontinent. In this struggle England emerged supreme and India came at last under the British.

During most of that period of Moslem rule, despite religious differences which made it impossible for the two communities ever really to commingle, Moslem and Hindus managed to exist side by side with at least some degree of tolerance, if not in complete amity. With the coming of the British, however, hostility and distrust between the two religious groups began to increase. The Moslems at first held aloof from the new overlords and were gradually reduced in importance, while the Hindus, so long suppressed, were quick to take advantage of the educational opportunities which contact with the West brought and to seek jobs in the government civil service and in the offices of English businessmen. In time, the Hindus became the more important, as they had always been the more numerous, community, and the Moslems began to resent what they felt was the favoritism showed them by the British. Bit by bit the

English found it expedient to grant the Indians some
measure of self-government, and growing Indian national
aspirations found political voice in the National Congress
Party which nominally represented all communities. But
the Moslems became increasingly distrustful of Hindu ambi-
tions and in 1906 as a counterweight to the Congress Party
founded the National Moslem League.

Many steps the British took in governing served only to
widen the breach now clearly formed. In 1909, for instance,
as part of a plan to increase further Indian participation in
the government, they introduced a system of separate elec-
torates for Hindus and Moslems, together with a device
called weightage, which gave the Moslems more than their
proportional number of seats. This meant that hereafter all
voting was along religious lines. As hopes for independence
grew firmer, the struggle between Hindus and Moslems for
political power grew more bitter and more frightening. Increasingly it was accompanied by widespread and violent
riots and reprisals for riots in which shops were looted,
homes destroyed and people killed literally by the tens of
thousands. Always it had been easy enough to touch off a
communal disturbance. A Hindu band had only to parade
past a mosque on a Moslem festival day; a Moslem had only
to kick a cow, sacred to the Hindus, and tempers would
flare. A melee of fists, stones, and sticks could turn quickly
into a full-scale riot that often spread way beyond the con-
fines of the village where it started.

By the time Lord Mountbatten arrived in India to work out a plan for independence, the strength of Hindu-Moslem hostility, the extent of communal violence and the intransigence of the Moslem leaders' demands—who warned they would never remain in a union in which Hindus were in the majority—made it clear that the choice was between Pakistan and civil war. Reluctantly the Congress Party leaders agreed to partition, for though they had hoped for a united India, they did not want it at the price of chaos. Thus it was that on August 15, 1947, India and Pakistan became separate autonomous dominions within the framework of the British Commonwealth.*

For Pakistan, this division of the subcontinent had an added complication. Not only was Pakistan itself separated from India, but its western portion (comprising the former provinces of Sind, Baluchistan, the North-West Frontier Province and the western part of the Punjab) was separated from its eastern portion (East Bengal and part of Assam) by some eight hundred miles of Indian territory. Neither was it a clean cut, for no matter how the partition lines were drawn, millions of Hindus and Sikhs still were left in Moslem territory, and millions of Moslems in the areas that went to India.

I have summarized the situation at this length—and, at that, far too sketchily—simply because it is against the back-

---

* India became a sovereign democratic republic in January, 1950, but elected to remain a member of a Commonwealth of Nations (the word British being omitted).

ground of these facts that we Americans must view the problems of Pakistan and India today if we are to understand the conditions that exist there and the importance of intelligent and effective help.

Karachi, on Pakistan's Arabian seacoast, was my introduction to this colorful part of the East, and an overwhelming experience it was. When I stepped off the plane I was greeted by crowds of officials beyond whom I glimpsed a sea of women. Other women in the uniforms of the various military groups of the All Pakistan Women's Association lined up to welcome me and hung around my neck wreaths of flowers and long chains of gold tinsel that ended in large, heart-shaped pendants. They were charming, but when you get enough of them around your neck they are rather warm and heavy.

While all this was going on, I could see out of the corner of my eye a rather extraordinary double-decker arrangement —a two-tiered stand mounted on wheels. Each tier was covered by a beautiful rug; on the lower tier was a microphone; on the upper one, swaying wildly in the strong wind, was a brilliant umbrella. Harnessed to the whole contraption were three camels. After I had inspected the military and shaken innumerable hands the Begum Husain Malik, my official hostess, asked me to step up on this affair. To my horror as I mounted the first level, and then with some trepidation the second, I heard someone remark: "I hope nothing frightens the camels or they may run away."

While I stood there feeling decidedly insecure, the Be-

gum* read an address of welcome and delivered a message
from her father, Mohammed Ghulam, the Governor General of Pakistan, who was not able to be there, and then
asked me to respond. I did the best I could and hoped that
now I would be permitted to leave the stand. But not at all.
I was asked to hold a press conference there. This really
worried me, because as I saw the reporters gathering around
below me I could not help wondering about the camels.
Also I was still very deaf from the plane trip; the wind was
blowing and I was sure I would miss most of the questions.
Luckily, the press conference lasted only about three
minutes, and very few questions were asked.

Finally I was allowed to climb down and was ushered
into an open car. I sat back comfortably, thinking: "Now
I can enjoy the drive to wherever we are going and get my
first glimpse of the streets of an Eastern city." I was wrong
again. As we emerged from the air field the road for half a
mile was lined solidly on both sides with camel-drawn vehicles filled with children of different ages. All were waving
American and Pakistani flags and all were shouting a welcome: "Pakistan *zindabad!* Mrs. Roosevelt *zindabad!*"
(Long live Pakistan! Long live Mrs. Roosevelt!) I tried to
bow to both sides at the same time, but that half-mile
seemed to me one of the longest half-miles I have ever
traveled. I know now how my husband used to feel on our

* The Mohammedan title for a princess or otherwise distinguished
woman.

drives through cities at home when I would keep urging
him to bow to both sides at once.

We finally left the camel carts behind and drove through
the crowded streets of Karachi toward the Governor General's house. It was a scene rich in color and contrast, swarm-
ing with people dressed in brilliant hues, with animals of
every variety—oxen, donkeys, camels, wandering freely or
plodding along heavily laden; with vehicles of all kinds—
oxcarts, rickshaws drawn by men on bicycles, and shiny
modern automobiles. But the houses, public buildings and
wide avenues gave one a sense of space and dignity. The
Governor General's house is set in a beautiful enclosed
garden that is almost a park, which we entered through a
wide gate. The house is encircled by roofed, open verandas,
and the rooms within are spacious and high-ceilinged. Here
I had my first encounter with the perfect service of the
British-trained Indian servants. They are almost invariably
men. I didn't see a woman servant throughout my stay at
the Governor General's house. Men care for your room and
make your bed. Men serve your meals and take your dresses
to be pressed. Apparently the purdah restriction which bids
women conceal their faces from all men except members of
their own families does not apply to servants, for the ladies
I met who observed purdah paid no attention to the
presence of servants—nor even, I noticed, to photographers.

The man in charge of the boys who waited on us at the
Governor General's told me he had taken care of my son,

James, when he stayed there during the war. That was before we had gotten into it, and my husband had sent James and another Marine officer on a trip around the world to observe and report on conditions.

Karachi was once a little fishing village, and as we flew in that morning I realized it was built practically on the sandy beach that seems to extend for miles around. During the last war it was an important port of supply for the armed forces stationed in India. When Pakistan became independent Karachi was made the capital of the country, though it did not then have the facilities in the way of buildings and accommodations that Lahore in the Punjab offered. But the Punjab was one of the provinces that during the partition process was divided into its predominantly Moslem and non-Moslem parts and the final line of division left the ancient Mogul city of Lahore, in what then became part of Pakistan, very close to the border. Unfortunately the bitterness existing between the two countries made it impossible for Pakistan to think of establishing its capital in such close proximity to India. Karachi, as the second largest city, with a good port, was the next obvious choice.

Some of the officials with whom I talked described to me the difficulties of those early days of independence, when they were trying to get the government set up and working. Under the partition plan, partition committees had been appointed to arrange the division of assets—plants, fixtures, office furniture, equipment of all kinds—between Pakistan and India, but at first the Pakistani officials found themselves living and working in practically bare buildings and hastily erected hutments, with completely inadequate equipment. They had no desks, no pencils, no typewriters, no paper, few telephones. They sat on packing boxes, wrote on packing boxes, and occasionally made them into beds at night. There were no files, no statistics. Karachi was unprepared to quarter the sudden influx of officials and government workers of all kinds, and there simply were not enough houses, apartments or even rooms to go around. Important government officials and their entire families sometimes had to live in one room for a considerable period.

There was also a serious personnel problem. Owing to the rioting that accompanied partition, train service between the two dominions was cut off and hundreds of Pakistani officials were temporarily stranded in India. There was—and still is—in any case a grave lack of the kind of trained personnel without which it is almost impossible to carry on the business of government. Under the British, as I have explained, it was the Hindus for the most part rather than the Moslems who went into the Indian Civil Service. Consequently after partition Pakistan had nowhere near enough people with administrative experience. A number of the members of her first cabinet had never before held office. Neither were there bookkeepers or stenographers or clerks. There were and are of course some exceedingly able people at the top who managed to get the government running; and many young people are now being trained intensively in various civil service jobs. Here the Ford Foundation is giving invaluable help, in India as well as in Pakistan; this is, I think, one of the most important of their many and diverse projects. But such training takes time, and in the meanwhile many of the top people in Pakistan are killing themselves with details that should be in the hands of trained civil service people.

The morning after my arrival I made an appointment to call on the sister of one of the two men who had been most instrumental in winning and launching the new state of Pakistan, Miss Fatima Jinnah. These two men, Mohammed Ali Jinnah, who founded the state, and Liaquat Ali Khan, who guided it so well during its early years, had become upon independence its first Governor General and Prime Minister.

Miss Jinnah was a dental surgeon by profession, but on the death of her brother's wife, a Parsee woman, in 1929, she became his constant companion, accompanying him on his tours, sitting on platforms at political meetings and, it it said, exercising considerable influence with him. Unfortunately, she was not well when I was there and wrote to my hostess, the Begum Husain Malik, that she would be unable to see me. Before leaving Karachi, I sent her a note and received the following reply:

Dear Mrs. Roosevelt:

I thank you for your letter dated 23rd February, which was delivered to me on the 26th. I am addressing this letter to you to the care of your country's embassy at New Delhi.

Thank you for your inquiries about my health. I regret I was not able to see you during your visit to Pakistan and fully reciprocate your desire to have the pleasure of meeting you someday.

Yours sincerely,

(signed) Fatima Jinnah

(Miss Fatima Jinnah)

Incidentally, I heard while I was there that an English writer, Hector Bolitho, whom the government had asked to come to Pakistan to write the life of Jinnah, had not been able to get Miss Jinnah to let him look at any of her brother's papers which are in her possession and which of course contain the basic material for a biography. This seems a pity, for the story of this strange, difficult, brilliant man should be written.

However if I could not see Miss Jinnah I did to my great pleasure see something of another remarkable woman, the Begum Liaquat Ali Khan. The assassination of her husband in October, 1951, shocked the world and was a cruel loss to his country, for he was a statesman of the first rank by any standards, moderate, firm and reasonable, and he had led a middle-of-the-road government.

I first met him and his wife in Paris at a meeting of the General Assembly and thought them interesting and delightful people, so I was now very glad to have a chance to renew my acquaintance with the Begum. She had not been able to meet me at the airport, for the period of mourning prescribed for a widow by Moslem custom was not yet over for her.

I found the Begum even more charming than I had remembered, a very interesting and lovely woman, whose two sons were with her almost constantly each time I visited her. The elder boy, a lad in his early teens, was very keen on photography and took some photographs of us all in her drawing room, and joined the press photographers whenever they were permitted to take pictures of his mother. The younger boy, who was about eight, was always at his brother's side and took great pride in being allowed to carry his paraphernalia. It was delightful to see such alert and interested youngsters.

During her husband's lifetime the Begum had worked closely with him, sharing his plans and hopes for the country. Together they had considered ways of raising health standards, of making more and better education available to more people, of developing improved farming methods, of starting the new industries Pakistan so sorely needs. She had been devoted to her husband and had admired him greatly both as a man and a statesman. Now she feels she must try as far as possible to further his program and still hopes to have a part in bringing some of his plans to fruition. When he was alive she, of course, had through him considerable influence, but now her own personality and actions have earned for her a fine standing in her own right.

It is because of her leadership and the example set by her and others like my hostess, the Begum Husain Malik, that the women of Pakistan have begun to free themselves of the restrictions imposed by tradition, to come out of purdah and to make a determined effort to be of use to their country in this period of its troubled beginning.

My hostess was a younger woman than the Begum Liaquat Ali Khan, and I think had been inspired by her to take an active part in public life. A lovely-looking person, and the mother of two small and charming children, she was always beautifully dressed in the costume of the Pakistani women—full trousers, tight at the ankles, with a long overblouse reaching almost to the knees, held in by a cord at the waist. She is really a remarkable woman, very much of a person in her own right, with great executive ability, tact and skill. She traveled with us everywhere we went in Pakistan, a most kind and delightful hostess, from the day she met us on our arrival to the day she saw us off at the airport in Lahore. It is still a mystery to me how she manages to fulfill her many duties, bring up her children so well, help both her husband and father and yet find time for her own outside work. I'm sure her children must have been glad when our visit was over and they could again claim some of their mother's time.

The principal instrument through which these women are

doing really magnificent work is the All Pakistan Women's Association to which most of the enlightened and active women in the country belong. This association has organized and made itself responsible for a wide variety of social service activities. It has set up clinics for medical care, established educational centers, arranged recreation programs for children. Through its efforts information about new and improved methods of agriculture is made widely available. It also encourages the development of various skills and crafts, such as weaving and glass blowing, among the people in the villages; in particular it has revived the ancient art of embroidery, not only teaching it, but setting up shops manned by volunteers where the women can sell their needlework.

At Sibi in the province of Baluchistan I saw an exhibit of this work, much of it so exquisite and so fine that I should think it would be extremely hard on the eyes. The rich vivid colors the women use are very striking; we might think them too bright, but they seem peculiarly right in that setting. Two or three women, sitting on the ground, were demonstrating the different types of sewing they do. I was impressed by the speed at which they worked under what would be for most of us rather difficult circumstances. One woman, I remember, held a baby on her lap, which she nursed as she continued with her work.

One of the projects the Association is backing, which was achieved largely through the efforts and foresight of the Begum Liaquat Ali Khan, is a College of Home Economics in Karachi. It will be part of a polytechnic institute made possible by a $1,600,000 grant from the Ford Foundation. Here young women will be taught how to plan their homes for greater comfort and health, and will learn the basic, practical rules of diet, baby and child care, hygiene and health. Others will be trained for various careers, as dieticians, home demonstration agents, decorators and so on. With the Begum Liaquat Ali Khan I attended the laying of the cornerstone of this new school which she hopes will in time bring a great change into the lives of the women of Pakistan, and through them into the lives of families throughout the country.

Another project that interested me greatly was a home for the rehabilitation of delinquent boys, where they are given both medical care and vocational training. It is very small as yet—there were probably no more than a dozen boys in it when I was there—but it is important because it is the first effort that has ever been made in Pakistan to treat delinquents in an organized institution.

All such programs as these, aimed at making life better for the masses of people, are at present largely a matter of private charity and personal social service. In time, however, I am sure they will come, as we have, to think in terms of what government itself should provide for all the people. Meanwhile the women of the country through the All Pakistan Women's Association are doing a wonderful job.

While I was in Karachi the Association held a forum for

my benefit with the Begum Liaquat Ali Khan presiding. One speaker after another discussed the various aspects of a Moslem woman's life: her traditional role, her present-day status under the law, her educational opportunities, the positions in business and the professions now open to her.

It is true that rules for everything that affects a Moslem's existence—from religious observance to the conduct of national affairs to details of family life—are laid down in the Koran, the sacred book of Islam. It is also true that historically women have held an inferior position in the Moslem world, and by the teaching of the Koran are lesser beings. Nevertheless, under the Koran a woman's inheritance rights are guarded and her rights in marriage defined and protected. For example a woman's father may make arrangements with her future husband for a specific sum to be settled on her in case of divorce; and if she is divorced, or if her husband dies, she is free to marry again. Moreover, though Moslem law permits a man to have four wives, it stipulates that he may not favor one at the expense of the others. (I gathered from the Moslem ladies to whom I talked that a trend toward monogamy was definitely indicated, since, under present conditions it was going to be increasingly difficult to persuade four women that they were all being treated equally well.)

It also seemed curious to me, considering how closely the custom of purdah is associated with the Moslem world and how completely the mores of that world are dictated by the

Koran, that the Koran itself nowhere contains any mention of purdah. The practice of secluding women apparently grew up in medieval times, fitting without too much difficulty into an existing social structure in which women had, in any case, unequal status. Most enlightened Moslem leaders today recognize it as a barbarous anachronism. Jinnah condemned it unequivocally.

It is too old a custom to disappear wholly overnight, but under the stimulus of the example provided by women like my hostess, Miss Jinnah, the Begum Liaquat Ali Khan and others, more and more women are beginning to take advantage of the opportunities that are now open to them. For they are not being asked simply to give up purdah, and offered nothing to put in its place. They are being encouraged to come out of purdah and to take an active part in the life of the world. It has been said that, indirectly, through their menfolks, Moslem women have always wielded a great deal of power. Now they are being encouraged and enabled to make their influence felt directly, on their own account.

For example, until recently only about 1½ per cent of the Moslem women could read and write. Pakistan's new long-range educational program includes plans for over six thousand primary, middle and high schools as well as a number of teachers' training schools and colleges. The government is also making provision for technical institutes and research laboratories, for scientific and technical scholarships for training abroad. These will be open to girls as well as boys, women as well as men. Already co-education is being accepted in the universities, where young men and women are given training in the same subjects, often in the same classrooms.

Women may now enter any profession and more and more of them are beginning to take advantage of this. Particularly, I was told, they are going into medicine. However it is very difficult to persuade any of them to go into nursing, which is most unfortunate, since there is a serious shortage of trained nurses in the country. Their reluctance is undoubtedly a holdover from the old idea of purdah, which forbade a woman to have any contact with men outside her own or her husband's family. Even though they may not observe purdah, they apparently feel that this is stretching their new freedom too far, that the men would not approve and would not consider them acceptable as wives.

I understand the reason for their feeling; nevertheless I kept finding myself protesting before groups of both men and women that far from lessening a woman's chances for marriage, a nurse's skills and training should make her much more valuable both as a wife and mother, for they would enable her to care for her family much more efficiently. I even told them what it had meant to me to have the training that a St. Luke's hospital nurse, Miss Lucy Spring, gave me. She spent many months with me when my children were babies, and saw them through various illnesses. I learned a great deal from her about the care of children and through her teaching became in time a very fair nurse with a sound knowledge of what hospital cleanliness meant. I was never more grateful for this training than when my husband was stricken with infantile paralysis on a little island off the Maine coast, where we could get no nurse. If I had not been competent to handle the situation, my husband's illness might well have been graver, and the danger to the rest of the family might have been more serious.

As far as the present nursing shortage goes, I do not know how much good all my talking and explaining did, but I am confident that necessity and the circumstances of modern life will in time work a change in their attitude.

Women in Pakistan have the franchise, another affirmation of equality of which they are very proud, and they are being encouraged to take on political responsibilities. As yet, however, many of them are shy about assuming their rights —I think perhaps because they honestly feel they are not quite ready, that this is too great an innovation and that they are moving too fast. So again in my talks before women's groups, I found myself constantly urging them to seize their opportunities. I told them about the League of Women Voters in our country, explaining the work they do here, and expressed my hope that similar groups will spring up in other countries where women have been given the vote.

While the emancipation of women is without question one of the really great changes that have come about in this

Moslem country, there are signs, too, that old customs and old ways of thinking are not going to be swept away all at once. In the hospitals, for example, the women's section is still served by women doctors. Some breaking down of the barrier is suggested, however, by the fact that on several of our tours of inspection, men doctors accompanied us to the doors of the women's ward!

In the streets one still sees veiled women, though I was told they are becoming fewer and fewer. Usually the veils are thin and light, but I saw some women in burkas, long, flowing, capelike robes that enveloped them from head to foot, with only small openings for the eyes. Occasionally I noticed a number of women clad in these heavy, warm garments, piling with their children into a rickshaw or pony cart, and a curtain drawn all around them. They must have been unspeakably hot.

The greatest change in the position of women has occurred of course in the classes where there is a greater degree of education. Yet many women of the upper classes, particularly of the older generation, whose husbands are prominent in the government or in business, are apparently reluctant to give up their secluded and protected life. My first evening in Karachi I was invited to dinner at the home of Khwaja Nazimudden, the Prime Minister of Pakistan,* to meet some of the Cabinet members and their wives. After introducing

* Replaced in April 1953 by Mohammed Ali, former Ambassador to the United States.

me to the various guests, the Prime Minister asked me to go upstairs with him to meet his wife. She, it seems, still observes purdah and so could not be present at a party attended by both men and women.

I found that she spoke very little English, so conversation was slightly strained and limited to my inquiries about her health and the health of her family, an expression of my pleasure in visiting Pakistan and my hope that I would see her again before I left. Her husband explained that she had been studying English, and had been getting on very well but had suddenly stopped her lessons because she was afraid that if she became proficient he would insist on her going to mixed gatherings.

Later, in Lahore, I called on the family of Sir Zafrullah Khan, Pakistan's Foreign Minister, and a man I admire greatly. Unfortunately he was away at the time, visiting Turkey and Egypt and other Moslem-Arab countries, but I did meet his wife and daughter. Lady Zafrullah Khan, an enthusiastic gardener, incidentally, is, like the wife of the Prime Minister, in purdah, and speaks no English. The daughter, however, has broken with tradition, and told me she hoped to come to the United States the following year.

While I was in Lahore I attended a large evening purdah party and at supper sat between two very sweet and gentle ladies who were more or less my contemporaries in age. I discovered, however, that they had pioneered in the cause of women's rights, displaying the same kind of courage our own early suffragettes showed. One of them told me: "I was the first woman in Bombay to take the arm of a British gentleman and go in to dinner unveiled. My family didn't speak to me for a year until my husband made my peace for me." The other woman had similarly suffered ostracism and disgrace for going without a veil, mixing with her husband's friends and daring to talk to Englishmen.

Together we marveled at the change that had taken place since then, commenting on how quickly, once the pioneers have opened up the way, the next generation can take advantage of what has been done and move ahead.

I myself have often observed that my children's generation seems hardly conscious of the fact that there ever was a time when women had to fight to obtain the right to vote and to secure various other freedoms we now enjoy in the United States. Even where they are aware of it, they do not really understand. Having always had the advantages the pioneers had struggled for, they are oblivious of the past. To see the same thing happening in Pakistan was very interesting to me.

After supper some of the younger women put on an exhibition of folk dancing, and then I asked for some Pakistani folk songs. These are sad and plaintive little tunes, sung in a peculiar tone that reminded me of our mountain ballad singers. Later I asked the dancers if they would like to learn an American folk dance that had come to us from England and that was still very popular. They were immediately interested, and so to Pakistani music I taught them the Virginia Reel. This was rather fun, for they were remarkably quick pupils and went through it the first time without a mistake.

As an aside, I might observe that the various purdah parties I went to belied the notion that women dress only for men. At least it is not true in that part of the world, for at all of the parties the women were most carefully and beautifully dressed and it was quite evident that they noticed each other's costumes.

A great motivating force behind the emergence of the women of Pakistan—a major reason their emancipation has progressed so much more rapidly and so much further than in the Arab-Moslem countries—is the situation brought about by partition and the consequent refugee problem. The need was urgent and immediate—and the women rose to it.

I had heard a good deal about the tremendous number of refugees in Pakistan and India—Moslems who had fled India and Hindus and Sikhs who had fled Moslem territory when the partition occurred—but the extent of this desperate mass migration and its tragic consequences simply cannot be comprehended until one sees something of the evidence with one's own eyes. It is known that altogether some twelve million persons were involved in the upheaval. For two untried governments, in the first days of life, a population transfer of this size created a catastrophic situation. The long-range problem for both countries was not the temporary care of the refugees, but how to dispose them permanently and get them started in life again. Many of them were farmers or had other usable skills, but to get them back to their old trades or to fit them into new ones and find them permanent homes was a tremendous job.

When I was there, four and a half years later, Pakistan had made remarkable headway in absorbing and resettling her destitute millions, though perhaps not so much as India, whose resources are greater. Incidentally, neither India nor Pakistan has ever asked for outside help in caring for these people.

Nevertheless, in spite of all that has been accomplished, there are still thousands and thousands wholly dependent on the government, penned in camps or living with no roof at all over their heads. In parts of Karachi and other cities I saw people, a barber or a cobbler perhaps, working in tiny temporary shops—mere cubbyholes—that they had been permitted to set up along the sidewalks, or even plying their trade on the sidewalk itself. Men and beasts were crowded together in dirty temporary shelters, which must have been unbearable in the wet season. That there had been no devastating epidemics speaks well for the cleanliness of the women—or for the immunity to germs that people have built up.

Even without large-scale epidemics, illness, malnutrition and bad sanitary conditions have filled the hospitals to overflowing. Infection at childbirth is frequent. I recall seeing one young woman, still in her early twenties, who the doctor told me had had six children, with accompanying infection each time. Now she had serious heart trouble and was lying there, her body half-raised, fighting for breath.

One of the refugee settlements I visited was fortunate in having a small health station to which a woman doctor came regularly to deliver babies and care for them and their mothers through the first few days. Here they were also preparing and distributing to the children milk furnished by UNICEF (United Nations International Children's Emergency Fund). I marveled at the difficulties the doctor and her attendants had to cope with. For instance, there was no electricity at night, so when a patient was brought in late they had to work by lamplight. The amount of improvisation and their efforts to find ways to do what should be done without any of the materials we would consider necessary were a tribute to their ingenuity and their willingness to work long and hard to make things better for the wretched people around them.

Pakistan must for some years give priority in her expenditures to increasing her agricultural production, setting up new industries and developing the power to run them. With so many problems, medical and housing needs have not yet been adequately met. Nevertheless, she is making provision for new residential areas and townships, for satellite villages and rehabilitation colonies for refugees.

Wherever new building projects are actually under way, in every instance they include plans for a hospital.

I was taken to visit one of these government housing projects near Peshawar and shown the plans for the hospital, the schools, the public administration building and various types of houses. I was interested to observe that though the new homes were of modern and convenient design, they still had the same mud-brick walls as the older houses.

In all, during the next few years, Pakistan is providing for 120 new hospitals, as well as 600 village dispensaries and a further 600 mobile dispensaries.

Before I left Pakistan I had several opportunities to talk with the various men in the government who were in charge of these and other plans for the country's development. During a visit to Lahore I had the pleasure of meeting Mohammed Ghulam, the Governor General and my hostess' father. A tall man of great dignity, he had recently been ill and as a result moved slowly and spoke with some difficulty. Nevertheless, during the course of our long conversation it became very evident to me how close to his heart were the problems of his country and how clear his grasp of them. Through him and the Prime Minister, Khwaja Nazimudden, and other members of the government I gained, I think, a very fair over-all picture of their hopes for the future of Pakistan and the measures they are taking to raise the standard of living. It seems to me that they are disproving the skeptics who doubted whether Pakistan could ever be a viable state. There is great ability and energy in the country; people have worked hard and are moving ahead rapidly, and using to advantage their internal resources and whatever outside help and capital come in.

Like all the Middle Eastern and Asian countries, Pakistan has been terribly handicapped by her lack of technical experts, people qualified to draw up, appraise and carry out the necessary development programs. To meet this need, the Pakistan government, the United Nations Food and Agricultural Organization, the U.N. Economic Commission for Asia and the Far East, and the International Bank have wisely collaborated to set up in Pakistan a center where this kind of training is available. Meant for the benefit of all the Asian countries, it seems to me to represent the best kind of international thinking and co-operation.

Knowing that Pakistan would always be first of all an agricultural country, the government has made its main object the increased production of food stuffs—putting special emphasis on those that could be grown for sale, like fruits, oil seeds and sugar cane—and other important crops. With five great rivers flowing through the country, and with the advantage of having incorporated through partition the fertile lands of East Bengal and the West Punjab, her chief problem, aside from further irrigation, has been to improve methods of cultivation, to supply better seeds and fertilizers and to make more use of modern agricultural machinery. Pakistan's own efforts have been supplemented by Point

Four aid and help from the Ford Foundation. When I was in Karachi, Mr. Avra Warren, our Ambassador to Pakistan, gave a dinner at the Embassy and afterward arranged for me to talk to Harry Knaus, our Point Four Regional Director there, who had just come from India. He was most optimistic about what Point Four could do in Pakistan and told me he was setting up four or five agricultural demonstration centers which eventually would help the farmers to increase their yield. Last July it was announced that under an expanded Point Four program over $20 million had been allotted to Pakistan for a rural agricultural and industrial program, designed to improve not only crop production, but such things as livestock and village industries.

The biggest boost to increased production will come from Pakistan's major irrigation schemes. We visited one of these, the Kotri Barrage, which is being built across the Indus River about one hundred miles from its mouth. It is one of the greatest irrigation projects in the world, with forty-four spans of sixty feet each. It is designed to control the Indus floods, and the water will be fed off to irrigate an area of nearly 3 million acres. They told me this will enable them to raise their crop production from the present 170,000 tons to 750,000.

We lunched that day in a tent right where the work was going on and then drove around to see the Barrage from all sides. It looked to me very like our own big river dams and development projects, and eventually, like the TVA, it will work an enormous change for the better in the lives of the people in the area. Five hundred miles away in the West Punjab another irrigation scheme is in the blueprint stage. Here 1,800 tube wells are to be dug. These, to be worked by electricity from the new hydroelectric plant at Rasul, will irrigate an additional 700,000 acres and help to drain the waterlogged areas nearby. Still another, the Thal Project in the Punjab, is near completion.

Some of the bridges and dams they are building have presented special problems, which occasionally were solved in an unusual way. I remember one bridge in particular, which they said had been extremely difficult to build because the flood waters had again and again carried away one pier. The engineer was in despair when one night he dreamed the pier should be in the shape of a woman's foot. Accordingly he built it that way and today, if you peer into the water, you can see it there, firmly planted on the bottom. No flood has ever budged it, which would seem to indicate that when a woman puts her foot down, she is determined.

Early next year Pakistan hopes to start work on an irrigation project in East Bengal, using the waters of the Ganges. Through a system of pumps and canals, they hope to bring 2 million acres under irrigation and make it possible to have a second rice crop in the dry season. East Bengal engineers and a number of engineers from the United Nations are now at work on the final plans.

These are all ambitious undertakings, not only in terms

of benefit to the country, but from the point of view of construction and the amount of money being invested in them. Consequently I was a little troubled when I studied the map later and realized that Pakistan has no control over the headstreams of the rivers on which such vast projects are going forward. The Indus, the Chenab and the Jhelum flow into Pakistan from Kashmir; the Sutlej and the Ravi come in from the East Punjab, now an Indian state. I couldn't help feeling that this put Pakistan in a rather vulnerable position.

The flow of water has, in fact, been a source of friction between the two countries from the beginning. On partition, India gained with the East Punjab only three of the original sixteen canal systems. This is an area in which extensive irrigation is essential, for millions of refugees poured in here and they depend on the land for a living. Pakistan claims that by diverting the water for her own irrigation schemes, India has reduced the flow into Pakistan, and that her vital canals are drying up. India attributes the reduced volume to drought on both sides of the border, and insists she is continuing the supply of water as before.

Some kind of international control of the entire Indus River system has been suggested as a possible solution, but Prime Minister Nehru thinks this is not a workable idea. For some time now, engineers sent by the World Bank, together with experts from Pakistan and India, have been engaged on a nine-thousand-mile survey of the Indus basin, with the idea of working out some kind of joint plan for its development and control. It is possible that with good will the two countries may yet develop a practical working arrangement for their common benefit, for as I understand it, there is ample water in the Indus system for both, if it is efficiently utilized.

Pakistan is also planning to spend a great deal of money over the next few years developing power for its new industries. I have mentioned the big hydroelectric plant at Rasul which has already started delivering power; another, at Dargai, will be completed soon. The other two largest, I believe, will be at Warsak in the northern part of West Pakistan and at Karnafuli in East Pakistan, both of them part of river valley development schemes. Through these and a number of smaller power stations they hope before long to more than quadruple their present total generating capacity, now one of the lowest in the world.

Pakistan still has very little in the way of industries, for here she has had to start almost from scratch. Nevertheless, she has made a good start on her long-range program. Cottage industries are being developed in rural areas—small, very simple factories where men and women from the neighborhood find occupation and a livelihood, weaving, making jewelry, pottery and the like. We visited some of these places, and while the equipment might be considered primitive, the work requires great skill and the things they were making were beautiful.

However, the cottage industries are only a very small part of the industrial picture. Many new factories on a much larger scale are planned and older ones are being enlarged. These include sugar refineries, cement, glass, chemical and fertilizer factories, and a big paper mill near Chittagong in East Pakistan. I know of at least one large, new sugar factory that has already been built, as well as a cigarette factory. The leather and shoe industry is well established. In Karachi and other cities I saw a number of impressive plants owned by Western firms like General Electric and Johnson & Johnson, besides many belonging to Pakistan industrialists. I recall particularly a large textile mill we visited; it was equipped with the most modern machinery and was running to capacity.

But the main emphasis in the Pakistan industrial program is on the manufacture of cotton textiles and jute goods, since jute and cotton are her two big crops, and the real source of the country's prosperity. Having emerged from partition with few textile mills and no jute mills (but 80 per cent of the jute-producing lands), Pakistan has energetically set about building its own cotton- and jute-processing plants and developing its own export markets.

Later in my trip, during a flying one-day visit to East Pakistan where the jute is grown, I saw a jute factory in operation. It seemed to me very much like a cotton mill. This particular concern was in the process of adding to its plant; it was evidently very prosperous and the machinery was modern, but there was no air conditioning. The air was filled with floating particles, but none of the workers wore masks. I was not surprised to be told that the incidence of tuberculosis was very high. When I told the manager that the people should wear masks, he said it would be impossible to train them to do so.

The houses in which the workers lived, like those in most of the villages, are built of mud bricks and consist as a rule of two rooms, with a small area partitioned off for cooking at one end. The roof extends over the courtyard, providing a kind of porch, and there are no windows —and certainly no screens. But though they are lacking in almost everything we consider essential for health and comfort, they are very clean, and there was great dignity in the way the people made us welcome and showed us their homes. Fruit and coffee were spread on a table under the trees, and nothing could have been more delightful than the kindness and good will expressed in their speeches.

My hostess that day was the wife of the Governor, Lady Firoz Khan Noon, who looked charming in a soft pink sari. Though she is English, she has become completely a part of Indian life. The thing she was most anxious to impress upon me was how much they needed in East Pakistan the kind of domestic science training school the Begum Liaquat Ali Khan had obtained from the Ford Foundation for Karachi. I hope indeed that one day her desire will be realized, for such a school is sorely needed.

I was deeply impressed by the enthusiasm of the Cabinet

Minister in charge of Pakistan's industrial projects. He has such a strong belief in his country's future that he managed to infect me with his own feeling of confidence.

In all of their various plans and programs, they are extremely insistent in Karachi that the budget be balanced. If they do not have the money for some particular project, they just do not spend it.

The shadow on the economic picture, apart from the high cost of armaments, is cast by the unhappy trade situation between Pakistan and India. The economies of the two countries naturally supplement each other; and at the time of partition it was expected that India would buy from Pakistan the jute and cotton she needs to keep her mills busy, and that Pakistan would get her coal (of which she has little) and cotton textiles from India. But the bad feeling between the two countries has interfered with this natural development; in the five years since independence, India has dropped to third place in Pakistan's international trade; Pakistan even lower in India's. India put a discriminatory surcharge on coal going to Pakistan; Pakistan levied an extra duty on jute sold to India. As a result Pakistan has been getting her coal from Poland, Czechoslovakia and South Africa, and selling her cotton and jute to other countries, notably Japan, from whom also she imports most of her cotton textiles. Japan, who is India's main competitor in the manufacture of cotton textiles, has thus become Pakistan's leading partner in trade. India has been buying her cotton from the United States, Egypt and Kenya and has been increasing her own jute acreage with a view to becoming in time independent of the supply from Pakistan.

Clearly such a state of affairs cannot work to the advantage of either country. It will not, for instance, help Pakistan to seek uncertain markets overseas, thus encouraging India to become self-sufficient in jute production, when she has such a large, natural and accessible market in this near neighbor. Nor will it help India, whose jute goods are one of her most important exports, to encourage the sale of Pakistan's raw jute to Japan, India's chief rival in this field.

I could not but feel that a trade policy which led each country thus to weaken the economy of the other, rather than to strengthen the economy of the subcontinent as a whole, was neither wise nor healthy from any point of view. But knowing there were able, devoted and selfless men in both India and Pakistan I felt that they must in time come to the point where they could acknowledge their need of each other. It was, therefore, most heartening to read recently that they have now signed a new trade agreement under which Pakistan has abolished her extra duty on jute to India, and India has removed her extra charge on coal to Pakistan. If this can be followed by a more general long-term trade pact, commerce may again begin to flow easily between these two natural partners, to the immeasurable benefit of both and to the world in general.

I am afraid that so far I may have given the impression

[87]

that my visit to Pakistan consisted only of a series of inspection trips. On the contrary, my hosts made every effort to see that I was entertained as well as enlightened, and arranged for me to witness a number of gala events and celebrations that were characteristic of the country. One that stands out in my memory was a breath-taking exhibition of riding and tent-pegging. Long pegs are driven into the ground at one end of the course; the riders line up far down the field at the other end, and then with spears poised gallop at top speed toward the pegs, attempting to spear them as they go by. We watched for some time from a little covered booth beside the field and came quickly to the conclusion that it was a daring and exciting sport. The riders were beautifully expert, and the Arab horses as intelligent, quick and dexterous as their riders, but with all their dexterity, the horsemen did not always succeed in spearing the peg.

Another day I was delighted to have an opportunity to attend a durbar. This particular one was held in Sibi in the province of Baluchistan, and a most colorful and picturesque ceremony it proved to be. Baluchistan, bordered on the north by Afghanistan, is rough, mountainous country, and the home of nomadic and sometimes unruly tribes. Once a year the tribesmen and their chiefs come in from the hills and gather to pay homage to the Governor and to receive from him recognition of their loyalty. It is an important and impressive occasion, elaborately prepared for,

As Pakistan Sees It

and attended by Cabinet members, military leaders and various other government officials, as well as plain sightseers. A red carpet covers the ground; under a canopy at one end sit the Governor and his staff; the rest of the people, under a canvas, are arranged to form a square, the tribal chiefs in groups facing the Governor, the guests along the sides. There is a mélange of costumes; some wear flowing white robes and turbans; others are clothed in a curious combination of Eastern and Western dress, and still others wear well-tailored Western suits. I was fascinated by the faces of the chiefs—strong, bearded, proud and dignified. The ceremony began with music; then the Governor presented each chief with a certificate of commendation and a small sum of money. The money is simply a token award to chiefs who have been able to control their tribespeople and keep them from making trouble during the previous year.

This business of tribal discipline is no small matter, and the significance of the award is only fully appreciated by those who live there and know how disruptive tribal raids on settled communities can be. As we drove about Sibi, before and after the durbar, and saw the tribesmen encamped on the outskirts of the city and even in the city itself, we quite realized what terrifying neighbors such young, reckless, warlike groups might be if their leaders did not keep them in hand.

I was very grateful to be given an opportunity, my last

afternoon in Karachi, to make a farewell broadcast to the people and to express my feelings toward them and their country.

To me, a Westerner, brought up to believe that church and state should be separate, a country where religion plays such a controlling part, not only in one's daily life but in the affairs of the government, must always seem strange. The very fact of its religious coloration inevitably limits and complicates its relations with its own citizens as well as with other nations. Nevertheless, the principles of Islam seem to me admirable ones for any government to follow. And I believe it is true that Liaquat Ali Khan, before his death, explicitly rejected the charge that Pakistan was a theocratic state. In the spring of 1950, following a resurgence of communal trouble in East and West Bengal, he and Prime Minister Nehru of India issued a joint statement accepting the principle that both India and Pakistan should be secular states, and pledging freedom of worship and full political and civil rights for all persons. A Constituent Assembly is now meeting in Karachi, its members elected by the legislatures of the provinces. The constitution it is drawing up will provide protection for the religions and cultures of all minorities—Hindus, Parsees and Christians, who comprise about 30 per cent of the population. It is expected that the Assembly will decide to make Pakistan a republic, but whether it will retain its ties with the Commonwealth, as India has, or make a complete break is not yet certain.

Whatever form their government takes, the spirit of the people of Pakistan is something one does not soon forget. There is courage and great vitality. They are determined to make their government succeed, and their nation a cohesive force. Any new government has innumerable problems, of course, but in talking to the men at the head of this one, I was convinced that their devotion and intelligent approach, with the resolute support of the people, cannot fail to make Pakistan a great country.

4

The Khyber Pass: A Sentimental Journey

There was one thing I wanted very much to do before leaving Pakistan and that was to drive up the Khyber Pass. Some seventy-two years ago my father had gone through the Pass during the course of a hunting trip in India and I had always remembered his descriptions of it. For me, this would be one of the truly sentimental journeys; so I was delighted when it proved possible to arrange it.

The Khyber has been called the gateway to the plains of India, a narrow cut through the mountains of the Hindu Kush on the border of Afghanistan and the North-West Frontier Province of Pakistan. It is the invasion route taken by the armies of Alexander the Great and Baber and Mahmud of Ghazni; it is the ancient trade route still followed by the caravans coming south from Afghanistan to India; and it was the scene of many clashes and skirmishes during the Afghan wars of the nineteenth century.

To get there we flew from Karachi to Peshawar, leaving

at seven in the morning. It was beginning to seem as if I were up early and late going to bed practically all the time— no one out there ever seems to mind early rising. The flight was pleasant and shorter than we had expected; and after an early lunch we started up the Pass.

The road from Peshawar leads west across a barren plain for ten or eleven miles to Jamrud Fort, at the entrance to the Khyber. This old fort is hewn right out of the rocks. It was here that the famous Sikh general, Sir Hari Singh, was killed during an Afghan attack. After his death, so I was told, his soldiers kept his body propped up at a window for several days so that the enemy would not know they had killed him. Later Jamrud was the garrison of the renowned Khyber Rifles, and the base of operations during the Afghan wars.

A few miles beyond Jamrud the road enters an opening in the mountains where the Pass proper really begins. As we drove through that narrow, winding defile, I kept thinking of my father's expedition and of how different it must have looked from our line of motorcars.

At the mouth of the Pass a number of Afridi tribesmen were gathered to meet me. I got out of the car to shake hands with them, and to my horror they presented me with three live sheep. I must have looked a little dazed as I pictured myself taking three sheep home with me in an airplane, for our government escort came to my rescue. "Accept them," he said. "Then they will be killed, cooked

and eaten in your honor." Greatly relieved, I accepted them
and made a polite speech. They told me some more tribesmen were waiting at a guesthouse halfway up, and asked me
to stop and greet them. I agreed and we drove on.

The scenery of the Pass is magnificent. Shale and lime-
stone cliffs rise a thousand feet high on either side, and
above them tower the majestic, forbidding mountains of
the Hindu Kush. All along the way plaques fastened to
the rocks commemorate the service of various British regi-
ments. The Pass is guarded by the Afridis, Afghan tribesmen whose home it has been for thousands of years. They
act as a kind of border police, and are paid by the government—formerly Britain, now Pakistan—not only to guard
the Pass, but to keep order among their own unruly tribespeople. The sentries are seldom visible, but one knows
they are there, spaced out at intervals, keeping watch from
nearby hillocks. Occasionally I caught a glimpse of a lonely
figure on the top of a high, rocky crag, bringing to my
mind Kipling's "Ballad of East and West" and the wild
chase of the Colonel's son after his father's red mare,
stolen by a Border thief.

There was rock to the left, and rock to the right, and low lean
thorn between.
And thrice he heard a breech-bolt snick though never a man
was seen.

Indeed, the headquarters of the British regiment that
inspired the ballad was at Mardan, not far from Peshawar.

After a distance we came to a high plateau from where we could see the fortress of Ali Masjid, the scene of many grim sieges, which commands the center of the Pass. Just two years before my father's trip, a friendly English mission to the Afghan ruler, Shere Ali, was turned back at Fort Ali Masjid, thus setting off the second full-scale Afghan war.

There are actually two roads running through the Pass in addition to a full-gauge railway: a road for automobiles and the road followed by the caravans. The Pass is so narrow in some places that one road has been cut through directly above the other. We were much amused by the signs at the intersections of the caravan route and the motor road; on the one, with the direction indicated by an arrow, are painted a camel and a donkey; on the other an auto. I was told that two roads were really necessary, for the caravans with their herds of goats and sheep and camels and donkeys are so slow-moving and often so long that they would completely clog the road and make it impassable for motor traffic. For the traders who come south in the fall to sell their furs and rugs and fruits, returning north in the spring, and especially for the nomadic tribes who, in the past at least, used to pasture their flocks in the Punjab in the winter, this twenty-two mile long pass was often a two or three days' journey.

On either side of the road wherever the land is level enough to permit there are small villages surrounded by high walls, each with its own mud watchtower. The farther up we went the more interested I became in the houses. Each house looked as if it were built to defend itself against its neighbor. In the outer wall, which is all you can see, are little slits big enough only for a rifle, behind which one man might stand and aim.

I had made a great point of being allowed on this drive to have time to see what we wanted to see and to take some pictures. This was the particular province of Dr. David Gurewitsch, my physician, who, as I think I have said, joined us in Israel. Today, for a moment, it looked as if his picture-taking might be getting him into trouble. He had climbed a rise at the side of the road overlooking some of the fortresslike houses in order to take a picture of one, when suddenly a guard appeared and leveled his rifle at him. We learned through our driver that the sentry thought Dr. Gurewitsch was trying to spy on the women in a nearby house, and he was vehemently sure that the camera the doctor was holding to his eyes was a pair of binoculars.

By the time this was settled and we had reached the guesthouse my curiosity to see the inside of one of these houses was keen. Lined up on the little lawn here were more tribesmen, with three more sheep and a large loaf of bread. I was asked to break off a small piece, salt it, and eat it, in accordance with the old tradition that whoever breaks bread with his host and eats it with salt is a safe and honored guest. Following this little ceremony the tribesmen presented me with a pistol made entirely by hand. It was a perfect copy of an English make—even to the name of the British maker.

While we were having tea in the guesthouse, I gathered up my courage and asked the man who seemed to be in charge whether anyone was ever permitted to see the inside of a tribesman's house. He looked a little shocked, but told me he would find out. When he returned to the room, he said he would stop our car on our way back and let me know if one of the tribesmen had agreed to invite us. I realized that to get this invitation would require careful negotiation and if it were offered, I could feel that a most unusual concession had been made.

We drove up the Pass as far as the Afghan border. The sentry houses were only a few feet apart, but we had been carefully warned not to so much as step across the line. If we did, they said, we might not get back again. Of course, there would have been no difficulty if we had had visas, but we didn't. Some American diplomats stationed in Afghanistan, who were on a motor trip, had heard that we were coming through the Pass and had waited there to greet us. I only hope they felt as much pleasure in seeing someone from home as we did.

We started to climb up the side of the Pass and Dr. Gurewitsch, who wanted to take some more pictures, was soon high above us. I thought he seemed in danger of getting over the line and rapidly sent a sentry after him before he was whisked away by unseen Afghan guards, who we were assured were constantly on watch.

On our way back down the Pass we saw some tribesmen standing beside the road, and though I saw no house, I immediately got out of the car. They led us down a path and we came suddenly to a house under a hill—just a blank wall with a door. We went through the door into a courtyard, where a little boy was playing with his goat, and then were ushered with great ceremony into a room that looked like another courtyard, for it had no roof. But a handsome rug was spread on the floor, and on a small table were set out the most exquisite china cups I have ever seen, filled with the usual black Arab coffee. I was so intrigued at finding such rare china in this rather poor and primitive home that after we left I asked about it and was told it probably went back to the days of the Czars, when much beautiful china was made in Russia. Some of it undoubtedly found its way into the caravans of the traders, from whom the people living along the route often bought goods. Today one could not buy such china anywhere.

The owner of the house explained that one room opening from the courtyard was the prayer room; the other was a bedroom. Curiously I peeked in. Against the walls stood three charpoys—beds with four low wooden corner posts and a wooden frame through which ropes are strung to form a support for their pads and blankets. The middle of the floor was hollowed out. Here in cold weather they build a fire and place a heavy, low table over the coals. A large rug is spread over the table and stretched out, forming a

kind of tent under which the men sleep at night, their feet
toward the fire. Hesitantly I asked whether we might go
into the women's quarters, and was told the women in our
party could, but not the men. The owner took us to the
door and then left us. There were two women in the room
and several children. At first they seemed rather frightened
of us, but after a bit they plucked up courage and showed
me with obvious pride where they baked their bread, and
where they kept their utensils. Apparently all of them used
the one room. Some pads and blankets were rolled up on a
shelf; and a few cooking utensils were arranged on another
shelf as decoration; but as far as furniture goes there was
none.

The court had one very amazing feature—a huge truck
built right into the bank that formed a wall of the house.
It had been beautifully painted with pictures in many
colors. I can only think that the house must have been built
around it; there was simply no other way for it to have
gotten in there. I imagine that at some point after they
bought it, it probably stopped running and not having
enough mechanical knowledge to fix it, they decided to
preserve it as a symbol of their riches and importance.

On our way back to Peshawar we stopped off at the
North-West Frontier University, and I had a chance to
meet and talk to the students. As always when I spoke
before university groups on this trip, I discussed the particular kind of educational preparation that was needed by

young men and women who are going to have a part in the modern agricultural and industrial development of their country. I would point out that in building a free and democratic government they were creating a model for their area of the world, and I would stress the responsibilities that this type of government inevitably demands of its citizens. Whenever possible, I allowed time for a question-and-answer period, for the authorities felt this might clarify the thinking of some of the young people, who, in the universities particularly, are subject to considerable Communist influence. But I shall have more to say about this later.

5

The Changing India

We landed in New Delhi on February 27, having flown in an Indian air-line plane from Lahore. Though I did not realize it at the time, this is apparently the only way one can cross from Pakistan into India. Trains do not run between them and all the railroad tracks have been torn up for several hundred yards on either side of the border. The only alternative to flying is to go all the way by boat from Karachi down the coast to Bombay. This is only another instance of the almost total lack of reciprocity between the two countries, a lack that prevents even the mails from getting easily from one to the other, that has shrunk the flow of trade and parted families. The deep-seated bitterness, like that existing between Israel and the Arab countries, has created a situation that is unutterably tragic, but there is no use in saying, as I have heard people say, that India and Pakistan should be and perhaps someday may be one country again. From all I heard and saw, I am convinced that Pakistan is completely established as an independent nation, just as Israel is. Nevertheless I can't help believing that the issues over which they are now so bitterly divided—water rights, Kashmir, the property of evacuated refugees, trade relations—can and will be resolved, given good sense and good will.

When we arrived in New Delhi, I was rather overwhelmed to find Prime Minister Nehru there to greet me; I felt that such a busy man should not be obliged to welcome guests. He was accompanied by a number of other officials, including Rajkumari Amrit Kaur, a Christian princess who had been a devoted friend and disciple of Gandhi, and who is now carrying a tremendous burden as India's Minister of Health; Major Yunus Khan, one of the President's military aides and Madame Vijaya Lakshmi Pandit, Nehru's sister and head of India's delegation to the UN. I was also extremely glad to see waiting for me Ambassador Chester Bowles and his wife. Many of the American officials who were so kind to me everywhere on this trip I had met before, of course, and it was always a pleasure to renew our acquaintance. In the Bowleses, however, I was greeting good friends whom I had known for many years; and since my stay in India was going to be so much longer than anywhere else, I felt great need of the advice and information I knew they could give me.

Madame Pandit had brought me one of the loveliest chains I had yet seen, made of cloves and other delicious-smelling beads, and I enjoyed their fragrance as they hung about my neck. Again, however, I had so many necklaces of flowers and tinsel that I finally took them off when I got into the car.

As we drove through the streets I was struck by the method of sweeping them. Old men and women, half doubled over, were swishing them clean with little brooms made of sticks or twigs tied together. And the brooms had no handles. I must say that considering what they had to use, they kept the streets remarkably clean. But there was a lesson in those brooms: In India people were cheaper than broom handles; it was easier to replace a worn-out human being than to pay for a handle for his broom.

We drove directly to Government House, the official home of India's President, Rajendra Prasad, where, as protocol required, we were to spend our first night. The following day we were to move to the home of the Prime Minister and stay with him for the rest of our visit.

In the days of British rule, Government House was the home of the Viceroy. Its last British occupant was Lord Mountbatten, India's last Viceroy, and, at the request of the Indians themselves, her first Governor General. Then, after India gave up her dominion status to become a republic, Government House of course became the home of her President.

I was given the room formerly occupied by Lady Mountbatten, and again, as in Karachi, I was impressed by the smooth perfection of the British-trained servants. I admit, though, that I was a little taken aback when my particular "boy" drew my bath, gathered up my dresses for pressing and was entirely ready to be a good lady's maid.

In the afternoon, just before the sun went down, we walked through the gardens of Government House—the most beautiful gardens imaginable. They were like some I had seen in England, only far more brilliant and luxuriant, and obviously tended by someone who loved flowers. The flower varieties were more or less familiar to me, but the blossoms were larger and more gorgeously colored. I inquired of one of the men we saw walking along a path (who luckily spoke English) whether the head gardener was Indian or English, and learning that he was an Indian, asked that he be told of my pleasure in the gardens, adding that I thought his color arrangements strikingly artistic. The man seemed most appreciative and was clearly pleased by my delight in the flowers.

We rarely saw flowers as we drove around the countryside, except where they were growing in carefully tended gardens. Perhaps that is because we were there in late February and March, for except when the rains come in the summer, most of India is apt to be parched and dusty. Then, too, the constantly foraging herds of cattle and goats eat every green thing; nothing really has a chance to grow.

As it happened, Lady Mountbatten was staying with the Prime Minister the first evening we were in New Delhi, and to my pleasure, for I have always liked and admired her, we met when my party went there for dinner. During the year she and Lord Mountbatten were in India she greatly endeared herself to the people by her warm and active interest in their welfare; and particularly by her tireless relief work in the refugee camps and hospitals during the partition riots. On this trip she was doing some work for the Red Cross, and planned to go on to the Far East.

During the course of the evening, I asked Prime Minister Nehru about an article on India's recent election, which I had read before leaving the United States. It described how people had spent days traveling through tiger-infested jungles in order to vote; how some of the primitive tribes had trekked miles across deserts, blowing little flutes, and announcing, when they finally reached their destination, that they had come to worship the god "Vote." Under the Indian Constitution anyone who is twenty-one and of sound mind can vote. There are no other qualifications, neither of sex, race, religion, literacy nor property. Out of India's 360 million people, this opened the polls to some 176 million. And of that number 90 million voted—more than half of them women, incidentally.

I told Prime Minister Nehru that I had been long enough an observer of political life to know that no great outpouring of voters occurs unless someone has done some remarkable compaigning, and I asked him how it came about. He beckoned me into his office and pointed to a map on the wall. This map told the tale. It traced all his campaign trips before the election, and showed how many miles he had traveled by air, train, boat and automobile—altogether 25,-732 miles. Not included, however, were the miles he traveled by bullock cart, on horseback and on foot. At the bottom of the map is a line reading: "The Prime Minister, it is estimated, talked personally to thirty million people in his audience."

Something of what this involved can be gathered from his account of an earlier campaign, described in his beautiful book, *The Discovery of India*. This was in 1937—ten years before India gained her independence—during the general elections for the provincial assemblies.

Toward the end of 1936 and the early months of 1937 my touring progressively gathered speed and became frantic. I passed through this vast country like some hurricane, traveling night and day, always on the move, hardly staying anywhere, hardly resting. There were urgent demands for me from all parts and time was limited, for the general elections were approaching and I was supposed to be an election-winner for others. I traveled mostly by automobile, partly by airplane and railway. Occasionally I had to use, for short distances, an elephant, a camel, or a horse; or travel by steamer, paddle boat, or canoe; or use a bicycle; or go on foot. These odd and varied methods of transport sometimes became necessary in the interior, far from the beaten track. I carried a double set of microphones and loudspeakers with me, for it was not possible to deal with the vast gatherings in any other way; nor indeed could I otherwise retain my voice. Those microphones went with me to all manner of strange places from the frontiers of Tibet to the border of Baluchistan, where no such thing had ever been seen or heard of previously.

From early morning till late at night I traveled from place to place where great gatherings awaited me, and in between these there were numerous stops where patient villagers stood to greet me. These were impromptu affairs, which upset my heavy program and delayed all subsequent engagements; and yet how was it possible for me to rush by, unheeding and careless of these humble folk? Delay was added to delay, and at the big open-air gatherings it took many minutes for me to pass through the crowds to the platform, and later to come away. Every minute counted, and the minutes piled up on top of each other and became hours; so that by the time evening came I was several hours late. But the crowd was waiting patiently, though it was winter and they sat and shivered in the open, insufficiently clad as they were. My day's program would thus prolong itself to eighteen hours and we would reach our journey's end for the day at midnight or after. . . .

Someone took the trouble to estimate that during these months some ten million persons actually attended the meetings I addressed, while some additional millions were brought into some kind of touch with me during my journeys by road. The biggest gatherings would consist of about one hundred thousand persons, while audiences of twenty thousand were fairly common. Occasionally, in passing through a small town I would be surprised to notice that it was almost deserted and the shops were closed. The explanation came to me when I saw that almost the entire population of the town, men, women, and even children, had gathered at the meeting place, on the other side of the town, and were waiting patiently for my arrival.

How I managed to carry on in this way without physical collapse, I cannot understand now, for it was a prodigious feat of physical endurance. Gradually, I suppose, my system adapted itself to this vagrant life. I would sleep heavily in the automobile for half an hour between two meetings and find it hard to wake up. Yet I had to get up, and the sight of a great cheering crowd would finally wake me. I reduced my meals to a minimum and often dropped a meal, especially in the evenings, feeling the better for it. But what kept me up and filled me with vitality was the vast enthusiasm and affection that surrounded me and met me everywhere I went. I was used to it, and yet I could never get quite used to it, and every new day brought its surprises.

He goes on to say that in his speeches that year he hardly referred to the individual candidates, and though he asked for votes for the Congress Party, his appeal was based on ideas. He asked the people to vote for the independence of India, and promised unceasing struggle until freedom was won.

Ten years later, as he again crisscrossed India, he must have been seen and heard by many of those same people. This time he told them that now freedom had been won, the next goal was an end to misery and hunger—better living conditions, better wages, more food. He explained what the government had done for the people during the four years since independence and what specifically it planned to accomplish during the next five years. But I doubt greatly whether any more than in that earlier election he talked much about the particular candidates of the Congress Party and the fact that he was the party's leader and that he wished the people would join it. Instead, I think he told them that in a new democracy such as theirs it was especially incumbent on each citizen to feel and accept a great personal responsibility; that the problems of the country could never be solved by any one person, but only if all alike shared the duties of citizenship. And I am quite sure he told them that the first obligation of every citizen was to cast a vote.

To make this possible in a country of such vast distances, where at least 70 per cent of the people are illiterate and 85 per cent or more live on farms or in villages, was a unique and gigantic undertaking. In the first place, the election had to be held at a time when the monsoon wouldn't make it impossible for people to get to the polling places; in the second place, it had to be spaced out over several months and held in different sections of the country at different times, in order not in interfere with local periods of sowing and harvesting. In order to have ballot boxes within at least reasonable distance of every population center (though we might not think it a reasonable distance) well over two million boxes were made and distributed among a quarter of a million voting places. Those who could not read and write voted with colored sticks, each color indicating a different party. The ballot boxes were marked with symbols: the Congress Party box, for example, was marked with a pair of yoked bullocks; the Socialist Party had a tree on its box; the Communists a sickle and ears of corn; the

Party of the Untouchables an elephant; and so on. That
the people are not particularly party-conscious, however, is
suggested by the fact that many of them, when asked at the
polls for what party they wanted to vote, replied that they
knew nothing of parties, but added "we want Nehru's box."
That the votes put into "Nehru's box" gave his party 75 per
cent of the seats in Parliament speaks for itself.

The first two years of India's independence were complicated, as they were in Pakistan, by the staggering refugee
resettlement problem. Much of the attention and energy
of the government had to be devoted to getting these people
under cover and started in life again. Since then the government has begun to tackle the other vital problems—
industrialization, river development, greater food production, education, health and the like. The country's needs
and potentialities were studied; her objectives set; and on
the basis of this an ambitious and complex Five Year Plan
was drawn up and put in operation. But there was so much
to be done, with everything needing to be done at once,
that I had a feeling that only a beginning had been made.

India is still a land of great contrasts, of a few very rich
people and great masses who have been poor and hungry
and oppressed for generations. This was dramatized for me
by the many pitiful little human processions that passed
me in the streets, where a mother was carrying her baby to
a funeral pyre. One out of every three babies still dies in
the first year of life in India. And wherever I went, it seemed
to me, almost all the people were thin.

Nevertheless, though India has far to go, she has made a determined and inspired beginning. This new democracy seems to evoke the kind of passionate devotion among its leaders that our forefathers had for the democratic government they were establishing here. Perhaps this is one of the greatest contributions the young democracies can make to the older ones such as ours. We have grown stale; we are inclined to take everything for granted. We find it hard to go to vote if it means we have to walk a considerable distance or if, because of the crowds, we have to stand in line to cast our ballots. Perhaps we may draw from people who ford rivers and walk miles of jungle trails in order to vote a new sense of our responsibility and a revival of our forefathers' readiness to pledge "our lives, our sacred honor and all our worldly goods" for the idea they believed would make this country a place worth living in. Not just a place where people could earn fabulous wealth, but a place where people could live in freedom according to their convictions and work to make their ideals realities.

The democracy India is building probably will never be exactly like ours. There is no reason why it should be, for her history, cultural background and needs are completely different from those that dictated our form of democracy and guided its development. What the leaders of India want and are determined to have is a democracy that is indigenous to their own country—not English or American or French or Russian—but one based on their own past and the character of their own people, and growing and taking form according to their own needs.

So far this has taken shape as a mixed economy. For some time the government will be devoting the bulk of its resources to the development of agriculture, irrigation, power, transport and social service; leaving industrial expansion largely to the province of private industry. However, the government regulates its over-all operation: If, for example, you decided you wanted to set up a shoe factory, you would have to get permission of the proper government board, who would then determine whether it fitted into the over-all, long-range plan. For the fact is that India simply cannot afford waste and duplication; it cannot afford an unnecessary shoe factory in an area where it may need badly a paper factory or a fertilizer plant.

It is in helping India to build in its own way and on its own strength that Ambassador Bowles has done such a remarkable job. I was glad to have an early opportunity to talk with him, for as I have said I felt a need of guidance. At that time, he had been in India less than half a year, but his ability to absorb background information and get the feeling of the situation is well-known. In those five short months he had made great strides in seeing that foreign aid was intelligently co-ordinated and applied. Perhaps even more important he had given Indians an entirely new idea of American officialdom, and a new confidence in our motives and our good will.

[112]

The Changing India

There is no use fooling ourselves: We must face the fact that in the years after the war our popularity took a terrible tumble in India, as it did throughout the East. In the Arab countries, as I have explained, this was largely because they could not understand our attitude on the partitioning of Palestine and the greater help they feel we have given Israel. We had always been friendly to them; these, to their mind, were not the acts of a friend. Pakistan, as a Moslem nation, is sympathetic to their point of view.

In India, after the departure of the British, the resentment previously felt toward them was in a large measure transferred to us. Never convinced that the British really intended to keep their promise to leave, the Indians were deeply impressed when they actually did, and the disappearance of their hostility was almost an overnight phenomenon. I do not think they have forgotten the long years of inferior status, or the economic damage the English inflicted on India, but even though they recognize that some of their present-day ills stem from British rule, their grievances have been swallowed up in a surge of genuine friendliness and good will. They tend to remember the good things the British did and to ignore the bad; and it is a fact that today the British are remarkably popular there.

However, having shaken off the domination of one foreign power, they are understandably determined not to fall under the influence of any other, whether that influence is political, economic or military. They remember that it was the establishment of a few harmless trading posts by the British East India Company that led in the end to the years of British rule, and they fear that American aid may have hidden political traps. Even Nehru, it is said, was at first wary of Ambassador Bowles's suggestions for Point Four aid, lest they concealed some attempt at economic domination.

American Imperialism and the Almighty Dollar is still a fearsome shibboleth in many parts of the world, particularly in the countries that have so recently become free. I think we suffer to some degree from history, for though we were never a colonial power, we were an adventurous nation: our ships sailed all the seas and our industrialists had enterprises all over the world. In the early days some of our business-men were perhaps none too scrupulous, and their dealings left a flavor that led the exploited black, yellow and brown peoples to lump us with all the other white imperialistic nations.

There are a number of other factors that enter into the distrust or resentment with which we are regarded in many of the Asiatic countries. We can all understand, I think, that no one likes the rich uncle who flaunts his wealth in the face of your poverty; who will help you, perhaps—but on his own terms; who will send you to college, if you like— but only to the college of his choice. This, of course, is not a fair description of our attitude; but, nevertheless, fair or not, it is the way many people see us.

In addition we have against us their feeling that we, because our skins are white, necessarily look down upon all
peoples whose skins are yellow or black or brown. This
thought is never out of their minds, though out of politeness they did not speak of it to me. They always asked me
pointedly, however, about our treatment of minorities in
our country.

We shall have to walk carefully for a long while to overcome these misconceptions. Everyone who lives or travels
in this part of the world will have to remember that he is,
in his own person, an ambassador; not simply an ambassador
of the United States, but an ambassador of democracy.
For the United States is judged by the behavior of its individual citizens; and to the people of these countries the
United States represents democracy.

By the time I arrived in India Mr. Bowles and his family
had, as I've said, made remarkable headway in dispelling
India's distrust of us and in changing the none-too-friendly
atmosphere to one of cordiality. I think that the impact of
the Bowleses on India was made largely by the warmth
they brought to diplomacy. Their life and their ways were
not those of the average diplomatic couple. They insisted
on moving into a smaller house, though there were those
who feared American prestige might suffer thereby. They
sent their children to an Indian public school instead of
to the school usually attended by diplomats' children. And
what is more, the children were not driven to school; they

bicycled. Mr. Bowles talked with innumerable groups of students, scientists and businessmen; he went out into the countryside and walked through dusty villages and talked and listened to the people there. Whether he ever got out among India's still primitive tribes I don't know; but I wouldn't be surprised. I do know that on one trip from Delhi to Katmandu in Nepal he went part of the way on ponyback in order to get closer to the country and its people. Mrs. Bowles, too, has traveled indefatigably, visiting American aid projects and interesting herself in the work done by the All-India Women's organizations and by the various charitable, missionary and semi-missionary groups. The children have made real friends. One Saturday morning I found the oldest daughter working in a small free clinic supported by the diplomatic group, helping to give out medicines and ladling out UNICEF milk to the children. When her parents came back to the United States on a visit last summer, she insisted on remaining behind in order to continue her work. In short, the Bowleses lived as they do at home, and approached people in the same friendly manner as they would their friends in Connecticut. By their essential democracy, by being themselves, they have made friends for America.

And that is the advice Ambassador Bowles gave to me when I talked to him. He thought that if I acted just as I would anywhere at home, the mere fact of my interest in everything I saw would help the Indians to understand

what Americans are like. His great desire, he told me, was
to see India realize that we—the people of the United
States—really cared about what happened to them. He
hoped to convince the government that our policies were
based on a desire for peace and that our day-to-day actions
were shaped with that idea constantly in mind.

The morning after my arrival, I went to place a wreath
on the memorial of a man who stood for peace in a way
few men have. Gandhi's *samadhi* is on the site of his funeral
pyre at Rajghat, a large open space near the Jumna River,
about five miles from Delhi. Here there will someday be a
park, and here the various nations have planted trees that
will in time give shade to those who want to walk there and
think about what Gandhi meant to the world. It occurred
to me that instead of simply planting an Indian tree, we
might try to find in our own country a tree that might
become acclimated to India; I think it would have more
meaning coming from the soil of the land that donated it.
Since my return I have learned that some countries have
done just that. Greece planted an olive branch there, and
Japan two rare varieties of cinnamon and camphor, specially
chosen as suitable for the climate of Delhi.

II

As I traveled about India the next few weeks the im-
mensity of the task this new government faces became overwhelmingly apparent. But I saw, too, wonderful and

impressive evidence of the courage and imagination and energy with which it is tackling the job of turning a backward and exploited land into a modern nation.

India has two problems that seem to me particularly urgent: One is how to grow more food; the other is how to control the rising tide of her population. There are roughly 360 million people in India today; the United States, with almost three times the area, has less than half that many people. Or put it another way: In India there are 280 people to the square mile; in the United States only 49. Even France, about a fifth the size of India, has only 192 people to the square mile. The trouble is that India's population, despite the toll taken by famine, flood and disease, is growing at an alarming rate. In the last ten years the increase amounted roughly to the size of the entire population of France. At the present rate—about 5 million a year—India will have a population of some 400 million by 1960. And even the elementary sanitary and health measures that are being introduced in the villages are bound to shoot up the yearly increase, perhaps double or triple it. If this happens, it would not be possible to raise enough food to give the people any more to eat than they have now; any increase would simply go toward feeding more mouths. So if India is to do any more than simply hold the line, if the gains she is aiming at in her development plans are not thus to be neutralized, steps will have to be taken to keep down the growth of her population.

The government is fully conscious of this and has had experts from the World Health Organization studying the possibility of introducing family planning in the villages. But it will not be easy. However, it is generally recognized that as a country raises its standard of living, the size of families is apt to decrease and the population tends to stabilize itself.

With the food problem looming so large, India has had to put increased agricultural production ahead of everything else. Right now, she spends $600 million a year, and more, importing food and cotton she could grow herself, simply to maintain the present inadequate level of diet and keep her textile mills running. I am told that with an increased food production of ten million tons a year—and that is what she is aiming at in her Five Year Plan—she would be self-sufficient in food and could then use the money she now has to spend buying grains abroad to expand her industry, build dams, power stations, hydroelectric plants and irrigation works.

I find it means more to most people, as it does to me, when figures like these can be related to individuals. In those terms, India's "grow-more-food" program would by 1957 give every person a daily grain ration of fifteen ounces —instead of the present twelve.

To achieve even this she needs not so much to bring more land under cultivation—though she is doing that too—as to get more from the farm land she already has. For instance, an Indian farmer gets only half as much wheat from an acre as an American farmer, and only about one-fifth as much cotton. Improved agricultural practices and techniques alone will make a tremendous difference: better seeds, modern tools, more fertilizer. (America's eight million farmers use sixty times as much fertilizer as India's seventy-three million.) To introduce modern methods to the farmers in the villages, India needs thousands of trained men—technical specialists of all kinds, agricultural chemists, experts in soil science, ecology, and sanitation, rural extension workers, mechanics who can repair implements, engineers to lay out irrigation and drainage works. The education the Indians received under the British didn't equip them with these skills. The British were interested only in turning out large numbers of subordinate government workers for the Indian Civil Service, which was perhaps the finest in the world at that time. But that particular kind of knowledge isn't what India most needs today.

Water is another problem. India's great rivers contain more than enough for her needs, but at present only a very small part of the flow is being used. Even with fifty million acres under irrigation—more than any other country in the world—only one-fifth of her farm land is regularly watered. The rest of the land is dependent on the uncertain monsoon rains which fall from late June to late August and rush off in wasteful floods, leaving the land the rest of the year as dry as a desert. To control and divert the waters of rivers and to make the fullest use of her rainfall India needs dams, reservoirs and extensive irrigation systems.

These are only a few aspects of the agricultural picture that India faced when she took over from the British—and they must all be solved if she is ever to grow enough food to feed her people adequately.

There is much that India herself can—and most assuredly is—doing to meet these problems; but obviously she needs some outside help. Happily, she is getting it. There are a number of organizations that are today working with the Indian government in an effort to help it realize its goals.

There is, for example, the Colombo Plan, a program for co-operative economic development and mutual aid drawn up by the Commonwealth governments with the aim of raising the level of living throughout South and Southeast Asia.

There is our own Mutual Security Agency (MSA), which works with friendly governments anywhere who need economic, technical and military assistance. Our Point Four program for technical assistance to underdeveloped areas comes under this; I shall have something to say later about some of the Point Four projects I saw in operation in India.

Then there is the Ford Foundation, whose funds in foreign countries are devoted primarily to creating conditions that increase the possibility of world peace. In India, supplementing the work of Point Four, it has established a number of demonstration centers and training schools for

the people who are to do agricultural, health and educa
tional work among the villagers, and is assisting with numerous village-improvement projects.

The Rockefeller Foundation is doing fine work in malaria
control, medical research and public health.

Under the UN Technical Assistance program, experts in
various fields are working with their Indian counterparts;
the United Nations Food and Agricultural Organization
(UNFAO) people there are making available to farmers
information on how to raise their crop production. For
instance, an international training center on soil fertility
has been established at the Agricultural College at Coin-
batore.

Health teams from the World Health Organization
(WHO) are helping with the elimination of malaria and
tuberculosis; the United Nations Educational, Social and
Cultural Organization (UNESCO) is giving India consid-
erable help with her adult education program; and the
United Nations International Children's Emergency Fund
(UNICEF) has saved the lives of countless children
through its supplies of milk and medicines.

One of the useful jobs Chester Bowles did as Ambassador
was to co-ordinate the efforts of these and other agencies
with programs in India. Where there had been a tendency
for each group to push ahead with its own particular job,
perhaps hoping to succeed a little better than some other
organization it considered a rival, now they are working

together smoothly and effectively—to India's greater benefit.

Even this partial list should give one an idea of what international co-operation can mean. It was vividly dramatized for me in microcosm when I saw the pilot project at Etawah where a great co-operative venture and a most encouraging demonstration of what can be done in rural areas is going forward.

Etawah is a district in the United Provinces, one of India's twenty-eight states. Here some 700,000 people are scattered among many small mud villages, which are usually only a few miles apart. The idea for this agricultural experiment was originally suggested by Albert Meyer, a New York architect who is responsible for many of India's new buildings and is designing the new capital of the Punjab. For the first two years the project was carried forward by the Indian government, which employed Horace Holmes, the Cornell-trained American agricultural expert from Tennessee, to head it up. Then, when the Point Four agreements were signed, the work at Etawah was brought under that program. Now most of the other agencies I mentioned are co-operating with the Indian government there. But Etawah is first and foremost an Indian project. We furnish technical assistance and advice, and supplies that must be bought abroad, on the self-help principle that is the basis of all Point Four aid, but the plan is an Indian plan and what has been done has been done by the Indian people themselves.

I was fortunate in visiting Etawah the same day Governor Modi and his wife had chosen to make an inspection trip, for I saw everything as it had been prepared for them, which of course gave me a much more comprehensive picture than I would have had otherwise. On the train I had the pleasure of meeting and talking with Horace Holmes. I found him a delightful person, enthusiastic and tremendously interested in the agricultural work that was being done. He had a great respect for the intelligence and dignity and fineness of the Indian people. His wife and family were out there with him, and I gathered when I met his wife the next day that they had done a wonderfully co-operative job.

It was an overnight trip to Etawah, and in the morning we were met with impressive ceremony. Before eight-thirty Scotch pipes could be heard outside the train; the Honor Guard was standing at attention, and a red carpet was rolled out. Promptly on the half-hour I was called for and joined Governor Modi and his wife in their car.

It was the beginning of a day full of interest for me. Mr. Holmes told me he had spent some time simply living and working with the farmers before he tried to introduce new ways. Then he did it by inducing a few of them to try something different as an experiment—perhaps imported seeds, different fertilizer or a better tool. When they saw the difference these things could make, they were quick to try them on their own on a larger scale; and as demonstration followed demonstration other farmers, convinced, began to follow suit.

Very wisely, Mr. Holmes and his Indian and American associates made no attempt to force drastic changes or to bring in heavy and expensive pieces of American machinery. They introduced simple but improved implements—a small steel plow, for instance—adapting them where necessary to the use of the Indian farmer. At one time the Indian government had imported some American seed drills. They were not complicated, but for some reason that no one had bothered to discover the Indian farmers had refused to use them. Mr. Holmes and his associates found out that the main reason for their unpopularity was simply that the farmers could not read the American figures that indicated the amount of seed to be used. After these were painted over with numbers the Indians could understand, they were delighted with the drill. The Etawah team is also training people to service the machinery, showing them how to improve their existing implements and even how they can make better ones for themselves.

They had prepared for us an exhibition of machinery for which they had collected samples of every type of implement, contrasting the old with the new: for instance, an old-style wooden plow would be shown beside a more modern steel plow, old knives beside new knives. There were also some very small imported tractors and examples of tools of their own devising—scythes or a simple but perfectly useful cultivator that blacksmiths had been taught to make from old automobile springs.

At another exhibit we saw a chart showing how they had more than doubled their crop production by the new methods now in use. We stood in the field of a farmer whose wheat was almost as high as my head. Realizing that it used to grow only about a foot high, I was not surprised by his enormous pride in his achievement, particularly since he knew it was largely the result of his own readiness to experiment and to work hard. That is the fine thing Etawah is doing: giving people just the little boost that enables them to go forward—and know they can go forward—on their own.

A number of the farmers also mentioned with pride the improvement in their cattle. Most of the cattle in India are diseased, scrawny animals and give little milk; but here at Etawah Horace Holmes and his associates have proved to the farmers the value of inoculations for rinderpest and Bang's disease, of introducing new and better strains. Where Egyptian clover was grown for fodder, the cows gave from 15 per cent to 50 per cent more milk.

India's cattle population is a real problem. Including water buffaloes, it amounts to something like one-fourth of all the cattle in the world. Half-starved, they roam at will through the villages and fields and farms, foraging for themselves. As a result the land is overgrazed, there is no fuel, and how many millions of tons of crops are lost to cows (and monkeys) every year can hardly be estimated. Even if healthy, they would be of no value, for most Hindus do not eat meat (many of them do not even drink milk). Economically then, the huge cattle population is a considerable burden. But their marauding numbers can't be reduced by killing them. In India the cow is a sacred animal.

So great is the respect in which they are held that they are allowed even to enter the village shrines and the houses. Cow dung is carefully collected, but instead of being plowed into the land as manure it is made into fuel cakes, which are dried on the wall or roofs of the houses. There, of course, it attracts innumerable flies; and since the houses have no screens or windows to keep them out, disease is carried rapidly through a community. In the villages in the Etawah district, the people are learning the importance of keeping their cattle segregated in shelters or enclosures outside the village.

Another effort is being made to get the people to put up small temporary privies which can be moved from time to time; in most Indian villages now there is nothing of the sort.

The village well, too—which is often no more than a scum-covered water hole—has long been a menace to health. Here beasts and humans gather to drink and to bathe; women wash their clothes in it and children wade in it. When I saw the cluster of animals, fowl and people for whom it is the center of village life, I was no longer surprised that the life expectancy in India is twenty-seven years, that so many babies die in the first year of life and that dysentery and other diseases due to polluted water are so prevalent.

Nevertheless, the memory I carried away after a day of visiting the villages in the Etawah project was not so much of the poverty and still backward conditions as of the great dignity of the people and their determination to build a better future.

In one village I sat and listened while a group of white-robed men, sitting cross-legged on the ground in front of me, told me through an interpreter what they felt the village needed to become self-sustaining. There was one tree to give us shade, and on a table near the tree was a small musical instrument, something like an accordion, which was evidently used at village celebrations. The heat was great; around us were the buildings made of mud. Just behind me was the schoolhouse, a long, low shedlike building with a hard-packed dirt floor which the villagers had built themselves. The children, who had been let out of school for our visit, were sitting on the ground in front of it.

As the men talked, I found that a great deal of what they needed was already within their grasp. They were not asking for charity, but only that water for their fields be made available, and the seeds and fertilizer that would enable them to grow better wheat. Given these, they would do the job themselves.

The Changing India

The Ford Foundation has one of its fine training schools in this area, where the young men who want to serve India by working with the villagers are learning from Indian teachers modern methods of agriculture, soil science, conservation and sanitation, how to put down a tube well, build an irrigation ditch, repair a broken plow or a hand pump and in general to do whatever comes to hand. Many of these men have already graduated from the universities where they took their academic training, for in addition to being jacks of all trades they are expected to become teachers who will pass on to others what they have learned, in a kind of snowballing process. Their hours are long and hard, for besides studying and working all day in the field, they take full charge of their own quarters and their own needs, and at night gather the men of the villages around them and by lantern light teach them the rudiments of reading, writing and arithmetic.

Yet the happiest, most alert faces I saw in India were those of the young men being trained in this school. Men are weary after a day's work in the fields of India, but these were a dedicated group. Their work was for India and her people.

At Etawah the people have learned the value of co-operation. The joint family system in India has always been a co-operative affair with the labor and earnings of all the members contributing to the support of the unit. But co-operation among the families of a village or among the villages of a district is new. Now they are discovering the advantage of pooling their resources, both in money and labor, to obtain for the village as a whole—to the ultimate benefit of each family—things no one family could manage alone. Together they are building schools and roads, establishing village industries, like brick kilns or hand-looming centers, putting in a tube well or buying a small tractor or steel plow that all can use.

To my mind the most important thing about the Etawah project is that it is not simply a brave but lone experiment. As part of its Five Year Plan, the government of India has now launched the same kind of integrated development program in fifty-five other areas, embracing about eleven million people in all. If they can keep to their present schedule, they plan to open more projects each year until by 1960 all of India's farm population has been reached. As at Etawah, the program covers every aspect of village economy—education, sanitation, health and home industries as well as crop production; and the aim is to enable each village to become self-sustaining within three or four years.

Very sensibly, I think, a large part of the $54½ million allocated for Point Four aid to India in 1952 has been put into helping her with this Community Projects program, on which a big chunk of her own budget is being spent.

India is spending even more on developing her irrigation and power systems, for without adequate water her farm program could not succeed. Point Four is helping here too, supplying experts and technical assistance. Present wells and reservoirs are being deepened and widened, and new ones dug. Plans also call for sinking about three thousand tube wells during the next two years to tap the subsurface water. We saw one of these being drilled at Etawah; each of them, I am told, will irrigate something like four hundred acres. These are in addition to the huge river valley development schemes for power, irrigation and flood control, which are along the lines of our TVA. Three of these huge multipurpose dams, at Bhakra Nangal, Hirakud and in the Damodar Valley, will by themselves irrigate an additional seven million acres. The first units of the Damodar Valley project in Bihar are already in operation; the power generated here will open up for development the richest mineral fields in India, and will feed the industries of eastern India. Up in the north in the foothills of the Himalayas the Bhakra Nangal project for harnessing the Sutlej River will reclaim many thousands of acres that are now arid and make them practical for refugee resettlement. It will also furnish over a million kilowatts of power to New Delhi and other cities in the region. That is almost as much as India's entire output at present. I did not see any of these projects myself but there is no question they are on a really gigantic scale. One of the dams over the Sutlej, I was told, will be almost as large as our Boulder Dam. And there are a number of smaller such developments under way as well —most notably perhaps, the mile-and-a-half granite dam over the Tungabhadra River.

Point Four aid is also enabling India to import fertilizer for her fields and to develop her own fertilizer industry. A new chemical fertilizer plant at Sindri is already producing a thousand tons a day. Other Point Four money is going into insecticides, jeeps, spray guns for the government's attack on malaria; and financing technical training for Indian students in this country.

I have gone into this in detail not only because I want to convey some idea of the really superhuman effort India is making—she is literally lifting herself up by her bootstraps—but because I find people often do not understand how Point Four aid is applied, nor realize that the money we furnish in materials and technical assistance is more than matched by the contribution of the country we are helping.

Faridabad, not far from Delhi, offers another heartening demonstration of the initiative and enterprise with which India is meeting her problems. Faridabad is a city of refugees, built for and by the refugees themselves. With its homes, schools, hospital, shops and local industries, it serves as a cultural and industrial center for the outlying villages. I was reminded of the rural industrial homestead projects we started during the depression, and learned that they were having to cope with some of the same difficulties we encountered, particularly the problem of developing industries in an area where adequate transportation is lacking.

Faridabad is being built and developed under the direction of a very remarkable man, Mr. Sudhir Ghosh, whose enthusiasm inspires one with confidence. A Cambridge University graduate, Mr. Ghosh had served Gandhi with great tact and intelligence as a kind of liaison man with the British during the negotiations over independence. Last spring he came to the United States and appeared before various Congressional groups to whom he described the work being done at Faridabad; he also made a thorough study of new community developments in this country.

To anyone familiar with Indian customs, perhaps the most amazing and encouraging feature of Faridabad is the fact that here people of all castes have been working together. The caste system has been a divisive force in India, imprisoning people in tightly restricted social compartments. Some castes have a religious, tribal or racial foundation; but in the main the four major traditional divisions are along occupational lines. At the top are the Brahmans (this is Nehru's caste), the priests, scholars and teachers; then come the Kshatriyas, the ruler-soldier classes; below them are the Vaisyas, the middle-class farm owners, traders, businessmen, artisans, shopkeepers and merchants of all kinds. This is the caste into which Gandhi was born. The fourth caste are the Sudras, the working class—servants, peasants and plain people in general. Each of these four large groups is divided into hundreds of subcastes and sub-subcastes, all having their particular occupational privileges and duties. Below them all, at the very bottom of the pile, come India's eighty million Outcastes—the people belonging to no caste at all, the Untouchables.

Caste traditions govern social life and behavior, as well as occupation. An orthodox Hindu of one caste would not, for instance, marry into a caste below his; indeed he would not eat or drink with someone of another caste. There is no way a person can climb out of his caste into a higher one. In the past, Untouchables could not drink from the public well, enter the temples or other public places. They lived in restricted communities and the children were segregated in the schools; even the shadow of an Untouchable was supposed to be contaminating.

Gandhi, as everyone knows, crusaded against Untouchability. He called the Untouchables "Harijans"—children of God—and made his home among them. Nehru has long denounced the caste system; its restrictions are ignored by many liberal and upper-class Indians. The new Constitution abolishes Untouchability and guarantees all people equal rights before the law. But, as we know in our own country, it is one thing to abolish discrimination in the Constitution and another to put it into nation-wide practice, and in India, particularly in the villages, it will probably be a long time before caste distinctions entirely disappear. Faridabad, however, proves that it is possible; here Brahmans, Kshatriyas, Vaisyas, Sudras and Untouchables are building and working side by side.

III

After our first two days in New Delhi we started by air on a trip that was to take us over a good part of India before we returned to the capital. At my request, and upon his warm invitation we had arranged a visit to the Jam Saheb of Nawanagar, who had on several occasions served on the Indian delegation to the UN, where he was much liked and respected by those who worked with him.

The Jam Saheb is the Rajpramukh—or Governor—of Saurashtra, an Indian state formed by the union of 217 former princely states on the Kathiawar Peninsula in northwest India. A number of similar mergers took place shortly after India gained her independence, when various blocs of princely states—some as large as a number of European countries, some less than a square mile—were consolidated into single units for the purpose of more efficient and democratic administration. At the time of union, one of the more important princes was elected Rajpramukh and a popular state ministry installed.

The Jam Saheb had at one time, in the days before India's independence, served as Chancellor of the Chamber of Princes, a consultative body made up of most of the rulers of the princely states. He is a jolly, friendly man, quite portly, who unquestionably likes and can afford the good things of life, but everything I saw on my visit bore out his reputation as an exceedingly intelligent and enlightened administrator. One rapidly acquires the conviction that here is one of the men who will play an important part in building India into a modern state.

Just to find ourselves in his fabulous guesthouse was in

itself an experience. It was more like a palace than a house, with verandas, wide corridors and enormous rooms. I had a sitting room so large I could not find where to turn out the lights, a bedroom and a most elaborate bathroom with so many fixtures and gadgets that I was completely baffled. I finally had to get someone to show me how to run my bath.

The Maharani is a charming woman and a delightful hostess, very quiet and competent, and in full control of her household and her servants—and incidentally, I think, of her husband and children. She has never accompanied her husband on his visits to the United States, but she told me she is looking forward to coming someday. She knows a great deal about cattle and farming and during her husband's absences she supervises the management of the property.

She has also made a special study of Indian medical lore, and gave me a book on Indian medicine which she felt contained much that might be useful in modern medical practice. Later we visited the hospital and medical school and library, in which the Maharani takes great interest, and saw an extraordinary collection of medicinal herbs and plants. One of the men we talked to here could neither read nor write, but he knew every conceivable plant and its use. We also saw their collection of old manuscripts and books dealing with Indian medicine and were presented with several very fine volumes. I was particularly interested in the construction of the hospital built by the Maharani and Jam Saheb: it pivots on an enormous rotating table so that the rooms may get the full benefit of the sun at all times of day.

Before dinner we were entertained by some charming and graceful dances performed by young women and children; and after dinner by another dance exhibition, but of a very different kind. We were to see many types of dancing during our visit to India, but this one we enjoyed especially. For this the Jam Saheb had brought in his farmers and some of the fishermen who live in the mountains that run down to the sea. I was fascinated by the dance of the fishermen— a remarkable rhythmic portrayal of rowing.

After the dances were over and I asked if I might thank the men for the pleasure they had given me, I received my first insight into the changes coming about in the caste system. The Jam Saheb called all the dancers over, but I noticed that only a few of the fishermen came. In translating my words of thanks, the Jam Saheb touched one of them on the shoulder, and afterward a government official observed to me: "How happy that man must be. It was probably the first time in his life that his prince has touched him." On inquiring further I learned that fishermen are Outcastes and that the prince probably would never have touched one before the stigma was abolished by the Constitution. That was also the reason so many of the group had hung back, thinking they still would not be welcome.

The next morning the Jam Saheb came over to the guesthouse to have breakfast with us and afterward we set out on a tour of some of the villages. They were well worth seeing. They were clean and well kept, and everywhere the people apparently had enough to eat. The women carried beautiful copper jars on their heads going to and fro for water, and the roads and fields were made gay by the bright, cheerful colors of their cotton saris. The cattle were segregated away from the houses; cow dung was not used exclusively for fuel, nor was it piled up on the roofs or against the walls of the houses. As a consequence there were far fewer flies than in any place I had been. In one village the people showed us how on special occasions they decorated their cattle with wonderful embroidered saddle cloths, bridles, painted horns and streamers of paper flowers.

We were shown several different kinds of houses. Those of people who were fairly well off always had a good-sized court and several rooms, one set apart for cooking, with comparatively elaborate furnishings in the way of carved chests, quilts and copper utensils. People of just ordinary means had two-room houses and naturally fewer belongings; while the really poor lived in one-room huts with a mud floor and usually only a door to let in the light.

In one of the poorest villages we saw, the people all lived in round thatched huts, very difficult to enter. The babies sleep in woven swings. I had seen these before in other homes, and a doctor told me that though they invariably make the babies round-shouldered, they are widely used.

However, they must outgrow this, for they seem to develop a good posture, particularly the women, who have to carry heavy loads on their heads. These particular villagers earn a meager living by making toothbrushes out of a stiff reed that grows in the vicinity, and they also raise a few vegetables in tiny plots.

At noon we returned for luncheon at the Jam Saheb's house, and then left most reluctantly and somewhat behind schedule for our flight to Bombay.

IV

Not until we were in the air were we told that the trip would take longer than we had thought because the pilot had been instructed not to fly me over the water. This meant making a considerable detour, and was a precaution taken for my safety that—considering I have flown hundreds of thousands of miles over water—was by no means necessary. Nevertheless, I could not persuade the pilot to disregard his orders, so our arrival in Bombay was delayed.

I was to attend a large formal reception and tea, given by the Sherif of Bombay, and, of course, expected to go from the airfield to Government House where we were to stay and where I would have an opportunity to change my clothes. I had on a linen dress and white tennis shoes which had been appropriate for my tour of the villages during the morning, but were highly inappropriate for a large and formal afternoon reception. However, on landing I was met by a number of officials who firmly told me that I must proceed at once to the party, so I went just as I was, feeling that it was more impolite to keep people waiting than to appear in the wrong kind of clothes.

When I find myself in a position of this kind, I remember how Uncle Ted (President Theodore Roosevelt) used to chuckle at Aunt Edith's ability to forget what clothes she had on when they were traveling in Europe and being invited to all kinds of royal parties. He told us of one particular occasion when they had been invited to dine with the Kaiser, and Aunt Edith's bags did not arrive. She had to go to the dinner in the traveling clothes she had worn all day but, according to Uncle Ted, she seemed perfectly comfortable and unconscious of any discrepancy in her attire.

It was at the Sherif's reception that, when I found I could not possibly shake hands with everyone present, I used for the first time the Indian greeting, putting my hands together in front of me and bowing, as I had seen the Indian women do. As we were leaving the hall where everybody was having tea, I was asked to go out on the balcony and greet the huge crowd that had gathered outside the hotel. Again there was nothing I could do except repeat the gesture as I looked down at the people, but it seemed to please them very much.

When I got into the car we could not at first get started because of the way the crowd pressed in around us. Finally we began to move and I stood up in order to see as many people as possible. The size of the crowds enforced a kind of stop-and-start-again progress, and at one point a lurch of the car made me sit down rather suddenly. The newspaper accounts of this made it sound as though it had been due to illness or overfatigue, whereas it was nothing in the world but an unavoidable loss of balance. At last we got out of the crowd and drove to Government House where we rejoined the others of my party, who were resting and cooling off before our dinner with the Governor of Bombay and his wife.

The first morning I woke in Government House and looked out I was struck by the beauty of the gardens and the landscaping in general. Bombay is beautifully situated on the water—actually it is on an island just off the coast—and its homes and wide streets are shaded by big trees of many kinds—jacarandas, acacias and other unfamiliar flowering varieties. Birds seem to be everywhere—green parakeets, mynahs, vividly colored chattering parrots. Here and there, built up against a garden wall or even a house wall, I noticed a number of little huts made of straw matting, the wall serving as the back. I thought at first that these must be the homes of refugees, but learned that they were occupied by gypsies, nomadic tribes or anyone who wanted a temporary shelter.

As we drove about the city, I noticed that the workmen carried little three-tiered lunch pails, and I was so fascinated by them I finally bought one and sent it home for use on picnics.

On another of our drives along the shore I asked to be permitted to board one of the picturesque fishing boats drawn up at the docks and loaded for a coast-wise trip. I should also very much have liked to examine the rigging of the sailboats at close hand—they seemed to have two sails, one very, very large—but this I never had a chance to do.

Bombay is the home of most of India's hundred thousand Parsees. The Parsees are Zoroastrians who fled from Persia at the time of the Arab invasion in the eighth century and came to India in search of religious freedom. They are perhaps the smallest religious community in the world, but their influence has been out of proportion to their numbers. Enterprising and quick to adopt Western education, they have had considerable commercial success and furnished India with many of her leading citizens.

Back in 1868 an Indian from Bombay named Jamshedji Tata, a descendant of Parsee priests, laid the foundations for what has since become one of the largest, if not the largest, industrial empires in India. Its iron and steel works at Jamshedpur, which little more than forty years ago was jungle, is one of the biggest in the world. Other Tata interests now include locomotive factories, factories where engineering equipment, machine tools, agricultural implements are made, cotton mills, hydroelectric companies,

Mrs. Roosevelt during a visit to Saurashtra, India, as the guest of the Rajpramukh, the Jam Saheb of Nawanagar (*shown at extreme right of upper picture*). *Below:* She inspects a thatched hut in one of the poorer villages in Saurashtra.

Above: The village of Jambuda in Saurashtra. *Left:* Mrs. Roosevelt is greeted by the villagers of Dhunwan, three miles from Jamnagar. *Below:* Visiting a gur-making center in Saurashtra.

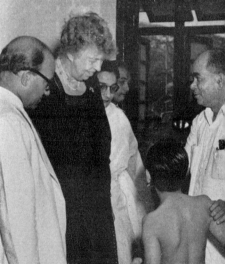

Above: Arriving in Bombay, Mrs. Roosevelt is greeted by B. G. Kher, Mrs. Lilavati Munshi, and others. She is shown chatting with a boy patient in the Orthopedic Hospital (*right*) and inquiring about foodstuffs at Annapoorna, the cafeteria of nonrationed foods (*below*).

In Trivandrum. Mrs. Roosevelt visits the Padmanabhaswami Temple and takes a boat trip on the waters of the canal.

Above: At the famous Water Gate of Seringapatam Fort, Mysore. *Right:* Mrs. Roosevelt makes a wish and crawls beneath the leg of the huge monolithic bull on Chamundi Hill. *Below:* She is seen leaving Somnathpur Temple.

Above: The Chief Minister of Hyderabad State greets her on her arrival. *Below:* Being taken around the Salar Jung Museum in Hyderabad.

Right: Admiring the wonders of the Ellora Caves. *Below:* A picnic lunch at the caves with her companions Dr. David Gurewitsch and Maureen Corr, and an Indian friend.

Mrs. Roosevelt and her party during their visit to the Ajanta Caves.

A dance recital held during Holi celebrations in Agra.

Above: The Maharajah of Jaipur, Rajpramukh of Rajasthan, India, greets Mrs. Roosevelt on her arrival at the Jaipur airport. *Below:* Later in the day, her companions enjoy an elephant ride.

Mrs. Roosevelt with Homi Modi, Governor of Uttar Pradesh, and Mrs. Modi at a village in the Etawah Project, where she watched a tube well in operation and was presented with a sheaf of wheat grown by one of the farmers.

Mrs. Roosevelt goes out on the Ganges at Allahabad, and makes the traditional offering of milk at the Sangham, the confluence of the Ganges, Jumna and mythical Saraswati rivers.

At a reception in Katmandu, Nepal, given by the Prime Minister, Mr. Koirala. *Above, from l. to r.:* Lt. Col. Sobachand, Mr. Koirala, the King of Nepal, P. N. Singh, the Indian Ambassador, Lt. Col. M. L. Thapar (of the Indian Military Mission) and Shri Upadhaya, Home Minister. *Below:* Mrs. Roosevelt with the King and Queen of Nepal, Mr. Koirala (*extreme left*) and Mrs. Koirala (*extreme right*).

Above: Mrs. Roosevelt being conducted in an academic procession toward the dais from which she addressed the Special Convocation of the Aligarh Moslem University. She received the degree of Doctor of Literature. *Below:* One of her most unforgettable experiences: a visit to the Taj Mahal.

Above: Addressing the guests at a reception held by the organizations of the All-India Women's Conference in Calcutta. *Below:* Prime Minister Nehru calls to bid Mrs. Roosevelt farewell at the conclusion of her tour of India.

Above: President Soekarno of Indonesia shows Mrs. Roosevelt his collection of modern paintings. *Below:* Stopping briefly in the Philippines, Mrs. Roosevelt talks with President Quirino at Malacanan Palace.

chemical plants, air lines and hotels—to mention only some of them. What I was interested to learn, however, is that four-fifths of Tata's capital is held by charitable trusts endowed by members of the family, and the profits earned on it thus go back to the people of India.

We visited one of their institutions in Bombay—the Tata Institute of Social Sciences, where graduates of Indian universities are given two and a half years of specialized training in professional social work, a service desperately needed. The Institute also maintains a child guidance clinic, where the students gather practical experience. Another Tata philanthropy in Bombay—although of a very different nature—is an institute for research in physics, mathematics and cosmic radiation and similar sciences; and in Bangalore they have established an institute for technical research. Another of their charitable trusts built a hospital that specializes in the treatment of cancer, others supply funds for research in various diseases and provide scholarships for graduate study abroad. Still other funds are devoted to social welfare and to the relief of poverty and distress wherever it is needed. The idea of the original founder, back when it was not easy of realization, was that Indians should supply India's needs.

One afternoon while we were in Bombay we were scheduled to go with the Governor and the Maharani to hear a concert by Yehudi Menuhin, who with his wife was also staying at Government House. Before the concert, however,

I had to attend a meeting with Madame Pandit. After I had finished my speech and while she was making hers I realized it was getting close to concert time, and began to worry about making the others late. But since Madame Pandit was going directly to the train after the meeting, it seemed rude to leave while she was speaking and not to wait to say good-by; so I sat nervously on the edge of my chair until she finished, then said my farewell and literally ran. Fortunately, when I got back to Government House I found that the Governor—who informed everyone that he had never in his life been late for any performance—had given me up and gone on ahead, leaving Miss Corr and Dr. Gurewitsch to wait for me. We got in just at the end of the first number, and enjoyed every minute of the rest of the concert. Mr. Menuhin played beautifully and was given a tremendous ovation. He pretty well covered India on this trip—we met him again in one of the southern cities—and was received with the same enthusiasm wherever he went.

The Governor's wife, Her Excellency the Rani Maharaj Singh, was much interested in the activities of the various groups belonging to the All-India Women's Conference, and through her I was able to see something of the work they are doing. One of their services has been to organize educational classes for the women in the slum areas. Often bringing their babies with them, the women meet in each others little apartments and sit on the floor as they study the rudiments of reading and writing. By apartments I mean one room, for in the city tenements no family has more. It did not surprise me that special classes had to be arranged for these women, for I had already learned in the villages that men and women study separately.

The most touching thing that happened to me during my whole stay in Bombay occurred when I went to visit one of these classes in the slums. A Bombay merchant, I suppose thinking it would not be fitting for me to see the rickety stairs leading up to the little room, presented the group with a bolt of white China silk, which was unrolled for me to walk on, from the edge of the sidewalk all the way up the stairs and into the room.

The same woman who was so active in organizing these classes had also started a restaurant where cheap but nourishing meals were available. Here they were also making an effort to accustom the people to eating certain unrationed cereals and vegetables that were not a part of their usual diet but that were a little easier to obtain. A number of similar restaurants financed by civic-minded groups have been opened in other parts of India, and must be a boon to white-collar workers on low salaries who must, nevertheless, keep up a good appearance.

The next to the last night I was in Bombay I had an experience that in retrospect is funnier than I thought it at the time. As it happens I am not very fond of bugs or spiders or snakes or mice; so before I got in bed at night I would make a thorough inspection to be certain that anything of this nature was outside and not inside the wonderful nets under which one always sleeps in India, and after I was in bed, I would carefully tuck the net in around me. That particular night, however, after I had turned out my light and been asleep only a brief time, I woke with the feeling that something light and soft and velvety had brushed against my forehead and hair. I moved quickly and reached for the lamp pull and turned on the light. Nothing seemed to be there. I put the light out again and tried to go to sleep. In a few minutes I felt something actually running over my body and I leaped from the bed, lit the light again and practically did my bed over.

I finally made up my mind that there must be a mouse hidden somewhere which I could not find. As it was very late I could not very well arouse anyone to inquire whether mice were apt to run over one in the night, so I decided my light would stay lit until morning. As a result I had very little sleep. The next day I inquired of one of the boys who seemed to understand a little English whether there were many kinds of bugs or mice that might come indoors. Smiling broadly, he said yes. I was not quite sure that he had understood me, but I was left with the rather uncomfortable feeling that they might come in greater numbers, and I still had one more night in Bombay. That night I took more elaborate precautions and looked everywhere before I went to bed. Perhaps I was too tired to feel whatever it was that was running around, if anything did; but after I put out my light I didn't wake up until morning.

I have to record that I never saw a snake all the time I
was in India, except in Agra where the snake charmers
performed for us. Then I had a feeling that the snakes
were doped. One of them started to make its way very
slowly toward us. I had watched fascinated as a cobra
swayed in front of the flute-player, but I had no desire to
be anywhere near them myself, and I was very glad when
the one crawling our way was captured and returned to its
basket. Handling snakes would not, for me, be an enjoyable
way to earn my living.

Before I left Bombay I had a chance to meet and talk
with the Prime Minister's sister and brother-in-law. Raja
Hutheesing is a noted Indian journalist with—at that time
at least—decidedly left-wing sympathies. He was one of
the people chosen to go on the official mission to Red
China, headed by Madame Pandit, to return the visit a
Chinese group had made to India. His selection seemed
to me a wise choice for he would go with an open, even a
sympathetic mind, and his report—the bad as well as the
good—would be credited. As it turned out, I believe, what
he saw in China changed his mind; for he found glaring
discrepancies between the extravagant propaganda claims
and the realities.

v

From Bombay we headed south for Trivandrum, the
capital of the state of Travancore-Cochin. This is the south-

west tip of India, and luxuriantly tropical country. As we flew down the coast I noticed what looked like a long lagoon or kind of inland waterway, such as the one that runs down our Florida coast. The water was dotted with numbers of fishing craft with huge nets hanging from the masts and little copra-filled boats covered with matting in the stern, propelled by a stern oar and a man with a pole at the bow. I decided then it would be fun to see something of the canal life, so when I learned on reaching Government House that there was no fixed program for the afternoon, I joyfully said I should like to drive through the country and go out on the canal in one of the little boats.

Trivandrum is charming, small, very clean and tidy, and its roads are bordered with tropical trees and shrubs. It is densely populated, however, so that driving anywhere has one unpleasant feature: You are obliged to honk your horn incessantly to clear a way through the crowded streets and roads. Very little attention is paid to the honks, but they do help to open up a path now and then. It makes things most disagreeable as far as conversation is concerned and you have an uncomfortable feeling that you must be making anything but a pleasant impression on the people you are shoving aside so that you may pass more quickly. However, nobody seems to mind.

We ended up finally at what seemed to be some kind of boat club. There were many interesting-looking river boats about, and I should have liked to go aboard one, but a rowboat and a motorboat were waiting at the dock for us. As we were getting out of the car, our local Indian escort suddenly said: "Madame is expected at a reception this afternoon."

I looked a little surprised and said: "Is there a reception? There is nothing on my schedule." Then, deciding it must be simply a social affair, I said: "It will not matter if I am a little late," and stepped into the boat.

The natives evidently were not accustomed to rowing, so Mr. Atal, my Foreign Office escort throughout the trip, and Dr. Gurewitsch took over the oars. We were out for about half an hour. Along the shore were little huts and swarms of children, with the peculiarly fat little bellies that tell of undernourishment. We saw more of the small copra boats and many odd varieties of birds and fish. I was enjoying it all thoroughly, but still I had an uneasy feeling, so as soon as we got back to shore I hopped out, told the others to have a good time and do anything they wanted to, and made my way immediately to my now frantic guide and said I was ready for the reception. Then haltingly he told me that this was a formal reception of welcome, given by the governor of the state. Again I had to consider whether I should go back to Government House and change into formal clothes, having already kept people waiting, or go as I was. I decided not to take the time to change; but even so everyone had been waiting nearly half an hour by the time I arrived—far longer than I had kept the people waiting in Bombay. I am sure they were annoyed, and I really suffered, but they were very kind and I felt forgiven after I had made my apologies. It was obvious that they had made elaborate preparations. Two children sang "The Star-Spangled Banner" and then the Indian national anthem. I was formally greeted and after I made my speech in return, I received the freedom of the city, written on a scroll contained within a beautifully carved ivory box. With each new attention I felt increasingly guilty.

That evening we dined with His Highness, the Rajpramukh of Travancore-Cochin. Travancore had seemed to me such a prosperous and tropically lush country—its very name means "Where the Goddess of Prosperity Dwells"— that I could hardly believe it when I was told that here too food was a serious problem. The arable land does not raise more than 40 per cent of the food they need and in the past few years they have suffered a serious drought. Coconut trees are their most valuable crop, furnishing not only copra, the dried meat from which coconut oil is pressed, but fiber for rope, while the inner shell of the coconut can be burned for fuel. Even the leaves of the tree are used to thatch roofs or are woven into mats or the broad-brimmed hats so many of the people wear.

They explained to us at dinner the unique and curious system of succession in the royal families of Travancore and Cochin. It has elements of a matriarchy in that, though a man is always the ruler, the succession is through the female side of the family. The Maharajah is followed on the throne not by his son, but by his brothers in order of their age. When there are no more brothers, succession passes to the sons of their mother's sisters—that is, the oldest male cousin. When these are exhausted, the sons of the next female generation take up the succession. Under this system a woman remains in her own home when she marries, and her children are supported by her family; her husband lives in her home or not, as he chooses.

We were entertained that evening with some of the most superb dancing and acting we saw on the entire trip. Wonderfully costumed and masked, the performers enacted an old folk tale—something like an early morality play—dealing with the sin of personal pride and its inevitable downfall. As in all Indian dancing and acting, every least gesture and movement has a special meaning and is carefully learned. We were told that no dancer, as the actors are all called, is allowed to appear in a play until he has had at least eight years of training.

The people of southern India are much darker than they are in other parts of the country. They are descendants of the Dravidian tribes who were living in India even before the Aryans from the north made their way down through the Khyber Pass about four thousand years ago. It is here in south India too that almost half of the country's six million Christians are concentrated. St. Thomas—the "doubting Thomas" of the Bible—is believed by many to have been the first Christian to come to India; it is said he landed on the coast of Travancore, converted many Brahmans to Christianity and built a number of churches. According to the same tradition, he died in India a martyr on his return from a trip to China and is buried not far from Madras.

Among her other distinctions, Travancore has the highest literacy rate in India—50 per cent compared to an average of 10 per cent for the rest of the country. More than 60 per cent of her children now attend school. Elementary education is free up to the fifth grade; after that one rupee a month—about twenty cents—is charged for each child in what they call the secondary schools.

In no part of India are the country schools difficult to furnish. One room contains all the classes, which are arranged by age groups. The children sit on the ground, each class forming a separate square and having its own teacher and a single blackboard on which the teacher illustrates the lesson. A few of the children I saw had slates—an envied possession—but most of them had homemade wooden writing boards—pieces of wood cut to the size of a slate, and rubbed and polished with grease and soot until they are dark and smooth. They have very few books, and what they have pass from child to child. Conditions vary of course from village to village; some schools may have only one teacher for all the children. Anyone who has seen the play, *The King and I*, will realize what teaching under these circumstances is like.

The Changing India

Under the British the rate of literacy actually fell in India. English was the official language; the study of English was emphasized in the schools, and preference in employment was given to those who knew English. It was an understandable policy from the British point of view, but it resulted in the decline of Indian schools and the study of Indian languages.

Now, however, as part of her Five Year Plan, India has drawn up a program to make education free and compulsory for all children between six and fourteen years old. This means she will need about two million teachers and thousands of new schools; yet despite the tremendous expenditure this entails at a time when there are so many other urgent demands on the budget, the present aim is to reach this goal by 1965. At the same time India is increasing the number of her high schools and universities and improving their standards. (At present she has twenty-eight universities, over four hundred colleges, seventy-four women's colleges and forty teachers' colleges.) To help fill the great need for technicians, agricultural experts and scientists of all kinds, she is enlarging her present professional and technological institutes (of which there are now about one hundred) and building new ones. The Indian government is sending some of its top educators over here to study the establishment of agricultural schools in connection with their universities and to explore the American educational system in general.

[153]

In addition, India is struggling to give its whole population a complete basic education through its provincial social service program. The aim of this is not simply to teach all adults to read and write, but also to give them instruction in personal and public health, and citizenship, and to give them the practical knowledge that will enable them to better their economic status. This last, aside from training in improved farm practices, involves a revival of the old arts and handicrafts—such as spinning, weaving, brickmaking and the like. To stimulate interest, they have recently begun using educational caravans, which travel from village to village, putting on plays and exhibits of various kinds, showing educational movies and distributing simple instructions which make it possible for the villagers themselves to carry out in practice what they have seen.

Both UNESCO and Point Four are working with the Indian government to forward its educational program; and, while it may be some years—perhaps even longer than they think—before all their goals are achieved, this is from the long-range point of view probably the most important project the government has in hand.

Leaving Trivandrum for Mysore, we made a detour to fly over Cape Comorin, the southern tip of India, where the waters of the Indian Ocean, the Arabian Sea and the Bay of Bengal meet. I strained my eyes to get a glimpse of Ceylon, but I could not fool myself into thinking I saw even the shore line.

[154]

Mysore seemed to me a very modern town, with many beautiful parks and wide, clean streets, bordered by well-cared-for lawns and hedges. Incidentally, the only tiger we saw on the entire trip was here—in a zoo.

The state of Mysore was fortunate in having an enlightened ruling family who also chose wise advisers. Under their administration it had become, by the time it acceded to India, one of the most progressive states in the country. It has many state-owned industries, extensive irrigation works, a good system of roads and railroads, fine hospitals, a high standard of sanitation—and like Travancore, one of the highest literacy rates in India. It is the source of most of India's gold and much of her iron and manganese and chrome.

In the afternoon H. C. Dasappa, Mysore's finance minister, took us outside the city to see the beautiful Chamundi Temple on the top of a high hill. Part way up the hill is one of the finest pieces of sculpture I have ever seen anywhere—the enormous monolithic Chamundi Bull. He is lying down, his fine head and chest well thrown back, and one front leg arched so that it barely clears the ground. If you crawl through the arch and make a wish, so tradition goes, your wish will come true. I did it, hopefully, but so far tradition has let me down. The rest of the group followed me on hands and knees, but I haven't learned whether their wishes came true or not.

From the Chamundi Temple we drove to the Krish-

narajsegar Dam over the Cauvery River. Behind the dam
are extraordinarily beautiful gardens and lakes and foun-
tains, which at night are illuminated in a display as gorgeous
as anything at Versailles. On the high ground overlooking
the dam is a hotel to which people come from all over to
witness the spectacle.

We drove as far as we could go, then got out of the cars
and strolled through the gardens, finally taking a boat across
the lake to get back to where the cars were waiting. Some
of the group, including Dr. Gurewitsch, stayed there to dine
and enjoy the cool air and the evening display; but I had to
get back, since the state government had arranged a formal
dinner for me that night. Mr. Dasappa and the other government officials who were escorting us never seemed worried about the hour, but the fact is that by the time we got
back and I had changed into my dinner clothes I was
again very late and had kept the other dinner guests waiting
a long while.

It was a delightful dinner. The orchestra was particularly
good and played a number of Indian songs which I thoroughly enjoyed—and, of course, "The Star-Spangled
Banner." This was always included, and occasionally
rendered in a way that made it hard to recognize; but I
appreciated very deeply the desire to do my country honor.
As at all the luncheons and dinners I attended, various
people made kind and pleasant speeches, to which of course
I had to reply; I often wished that I had my husband's
facility for making apt and charming responses.

[156]

Early the next morning I went to speak to the students at Mysore University, and then visited the Rockefeller Foundation Research Institute. The director was away but we talked to Dr. Richmond K. Anderson who is in charge of the medical research being done there. As I think I have said, the Rockefeller people are doing wonderful work in India in malaria control; and they also have an excellent training program for public health workers. In addition, the Foundation gives fellowships to students for training abroad, and makes travel grants to public health officers for visits to Europe and the United States and other parts of India. I gathered, though, from talking to Dr. Anderson that the number of trained workers is still desperately small and must be multiplied many, many times before a really effective and over-all attack can be made on India's public health problems.

When we left Mysore we were accompanied by Mr. Dasappa, who took us on a sight-seeing tour that was to end up in Bangalore. One of the most interesting things we saw, from a historical point of view, was the old fort at Seringapatam, where the great Moslem general, Tippoo Sahib, was finally defeated by the British in 1799. Tippoo's father, Hyder Ali, who was also a great military commander, had seized control of Mysore from the ruling Hindu family and had made himself Maharajah. This was the period when the British and French were still contesting for supremacy in India, and Hyder Ali generally sided with the French, at the same time enlarging his own territory. He defeated the English in a number of battles, but was beaten by Warren Hastings when he tried to conquer Madras. After he died his son Tippoo succeeded him, and in turn was defeated by Cornwallis—the same Cornwallis who had earlier led the English armies against George Washington—when he invaded Travancore. His last battle against the British was fought at Seringapatam, where he was killed defending his capital. We were shown the place where the British and their Indian allies were finally able to force an entrance to the fort. The walls of the fort are several feet thick, but there had to be an opening through which the people inside could go out to get water. At this point, the Water Gate, the defense was vulnerable; the British discovered the weakness, and here they made their entry. After the battle, Wellington—then Colonel Wellesley—was put in command of the fort, and the Hindu rulers were restored to power.

Before we started out that morning, knowing we had some distance to cover and would be traveling dirt roads most of the way, I had suggested that we take a picnic lunch with us instead of stopping at a restaurant. India seemed to me a place where picnicking should be a familiar form of entertainment to everyone; but I realized later that most of the year it is much too hot to make eating out-of-doors enjoyable; then too, I suppose, there is some danger from snakes and poisonous insects. However, I had given no thought to this, nor to the fact that Indian food, unlike sandwiches, is not easily packed, but my hosts were kind enough to accede to my wish. It turned out to be not quite the kind of picnic lunch I had expected. We stopped at an exquisite Hindu temple—Somnathpur—beautifully carved around the base and completely surrounded by a lovely old colonnade. Happily I heard someone suggest that we eat there under the colonnade, and then to my surprise I immediately saw tables being set up, hampers being unpacked and waiters running back and forth. My picnic was just an elaborate meal out-of-doors. However, in those unique surroundings, we enjoyed our meal very much and time slipped by so fast we were late in leaving. Further on we stopped again to look at the mosque of Jumma Masjid, which is distinguished not only by its beautiful carvings but by the fact that it has two minarets built close together. Ordinarily the minarets are at the corners of the surrounding square.

Everywhere and in all sorts of ways as I traveled about India I was conscious of traces of the British influence—in the gardens, in the buildings, in the customs, in the historical markers noting the service of various British generals or statesmen. Many who later achieved great distinction or the highest possible military rank had their early training in India. Architectural styles, a palace in Bangalore that is a copy of a small section of Windsor Castle, looking very out of place, a garden laid out by the same gardener who laid out the gardens in Kew, near London, the habit of dining at eight or eight-thirty, of dressing for dinner, the popularity of certain English sports, the use of English as the official language—such things as these attest to the fact that the British once conquered and occupied the country.

But at the same time I kept being impressed by how little real depth there was to this influence. The buildings, when all is said and done, had to be adapted to the climate of India and so, despite traces of British taste, are basically Indian in feeling and style. British customs prevail chiefly among the upper classes—they haven't affected the way of life of the majority; most of India's millions speak some form of one of her fifteen different languages and have little or no knowledge of English. In short, I do not think that the occupation changed India fundamentally, nor did it create any deep understanding between the English and the Indians. The Indians who went to England for their education, as many of the wealthy and intellectual classes did, tried while they were there to be as much like the English as possible; but it was an outward conformance. They did not really change inside. It was characteristic of the British to assume that this outward observance of manners, customs and habits implied an inner acceptance and belief. They are so convinced themselves that what they do is right and their way of doing it preferable to any other way that only here and there do you find an exceptional Britisher who can project himself into the minds and feelings of the people of a different race. For all the years of occupation, they didn't change the soul and the spirit of India, and even the most Anglicized of the Indians are still fundamentally Indian and not British.

VI

All through my trip I had been hearing of the dreadful famine conditions in the whole Madras area where, after six years of drought, people were experiencing indescribable hunger. The lucky ones were being kept alive on one little bowl of gruel a day; others even boiled leaves to stay the pangs of hunger. I had intended going there from Bangalore, but I had begun to feel somewhat weary; also the constant flying had affected my ears. They were bothering me considerably, and I was deaf for a longer period after each flight. My itinerary had been so planned that I would have had to go far to the north and then return to Madras, which would have meant many more hours of air travel. Reluctantly I decided it would be wiser to travel at a more leisurely pace, so we went directly to Hyderabad.

Hyderabad is one of the former princely states which enjoyed a treaty relationship with Great Britain, whom it recognized as the paramount power. It is governed by the Nizam of Hyderabad (now the Rajpramukh), or to give him his full title: His Exalted Highness Mir Osman Ali Khan, Asaf Jah VII, Nizam of Hyderabad and Berar. A legendary figure of enormous wealth and parsimonious habits, he had ruled Hyderabad almost as an Oriental potentate with vast powers over his subjects. I was told that he had an eye for the ladies, and when visiting would frequently suggest that he would like to take one of his host's daughters—usually a particularly attractive one— under his protection, and ask that she be sent to the palace. This often meant that the young lady was never seen again.

At the time India became independent, and the princely states were, in effect, given the choice of joining either India or Pakistan, the Nizam stalled and dillydallied. A devout Moslem, and a direct descendant of the Mogul Emperor's Viceroy, he had no desire to come under the control of Hindu India—even though 86 per cent of his subjects were Hindus. Actually he wanted to be an independent monarch, with Hyderabad as his private and separate domain. However, anyone who studies the situation of Hyderabad, in the very heart of India, can see how impossible this was. Its geographical position, its overwhelming Hindu population, the fact that, though one of the largest and richest states in the country, it was by no means self-sustaining, meant that its interests and its very life were inextricably bound up with India's. Nevertheless the Nizam continued to procrastinate for a year, while relations between Hyderabad and India grew steadily more tense. Not until September, 1948, after a show of power and a "police action" on the part of India, did he finally give in and bring Hyderabad into the Indian union.

The Changing India

Mr. Vellodi, our host while we were there, is an adviser to the Chief Minister of the state. His wife, an active member of the All-India Women's Conference, is, as I quickly found, keenly alive to the social and economic problems of India and one of the many women I was fortunate in meeting who recognized that they must assume a share of the responsibility for solving them.

The first day we spent in Hyderabad was the beginning of the Holi carnival, an ancient Indian festival when people gather in the streets and throw brightly colored dyes at one another. I understand that the dyes are made of talc tinted with a color and mixed with crushed mica; whatever their compostion they are most effective: the streets, people's clothes and hair and skin are brilliantly stained for several days. This first day of Holi the fun seemed fairly mild and most of the participants were young people. Nevertheless, having no spare clothes to throw away, we took no chances and tried to stay out of the way of the revelers.

We drove through different parts of the city, and occasionally got out and walked, taking pictures and looking into shop windows. This I discovered later was an unheard of procedure for a lady; she is supposed to stay in her car or carriage and have the shopkeeper bring out to her whatever she wishes to see. We strolled down the street of the silversmiths, looking at their wares, down a street where all the lovely tinsel ornaments are made, and along another street where beautiful silk embroidery is done. I was told

[163]

that the people who do this exquisite work never use a pattern; they know the designs so well they do not need to trace them on the material.

Hyderabad is a walled city with, I believe, eight gates. Toward the end of the day we visited one part of the fortifications surrounding the old capital. The light as the sun set and the moon rose on the walls gave the scene a fairyland look, and we climbed up inside the fort and stood on the top of a wall that looked over the great plains. The next day we went back and saw the main gate whose heavy doors are studded with iron spikes. In the days when the fort was built, back in the sixteenth century, elephants were often used in battle, and during an attack acted as battering rams to break down the doors of a fort. The purpose of the iron spikes was to discourage them from making this kind of charge.

As you come through the doors, there is a kind of archway leading both to the right and to the left; either way takes you eventually to the top of the hill and the last fortress inside the outer walls. Any horse or even person passing through the arch creates an echo which can be heard on top of the hill; this in the old days served to warn the emperor or his generals of the approach of either friend or foe.

We stopped at a large bathing pool which is the water supply for the people of the villages inside the walls, and where they also immerse themselves before performing their religious rites. If you give a shout at the entrance to the pool, here too an echo comes back three times from the top of the hill.

At the end of the morning we lunched with the Prince of Berar, the Nizam's heir. He is a youngish man and rather stout. His wife spends much of her time in England with their two sons, who are being educated there. The Prince seems pleasant, but not particularly interested in anything beyond his own affairs and surroundings. I rather doubt whether he will develop into one of India's liberal leaders, but it is always difficult to be sure until a man has had an opportunity to give expression to his own interests. I suspect that under his father the Prince is not in a position to do much on his own.

During lunch I had to leave the table for a press conference, which was quite a nuisance. However, this seemed to mean a great deal to the newspaper people everywhere I stopped, so I always tried to give them an opportunity to question me.

VII

It was almost the middle of March when we arrived in Aurangabad, after a rather bumpy flight, to begin an interlude of several days for which I had no social engagements at all, and planned only to see something of India's sculptural treasures. Aurangabad is in the northwest part of the state of Hyderabad, not far from the little village that is the site of the famous Ellora Caves. These are a series of rock and cave temples and monasteries that extend for a mile on the side of a hill. They were literally hewn out of solid rock by Brahman, Buddhist and Jain monks during the seventh and eighth centuries. I had previously seen some wonderful pictures of the caves in a book Yehudi Menuhin had allowed us to look over in Bombay, but they did not in any way convey their real majesty. No pictures, no words, could do justice to the work that has been done there. When you arrive at the caves you are face to face with a wall of rock in which there are a number of openings. As you enter one you feel you must be going straight into the mountainside, but once within you can look up at the sky. Around the sides of the first cave is a gallery cut out of the rock and in the center is a huge temple that was carved out of a single mass of stone. On either side of the entrance are two great elephants and two tall columns, and the roof of the central hall is supported by sixteen square pillars. All around the temple, on all the surfaces and on the galleries of the cave, are carved friezes showing mythological figures and animals, or scenes of domestic life and worship. In all the caves of the Buddhist and Jain groups (there are something like thirty-four caves in all, I believe) were many carved figures of Buddha and of Mahavira (the principal saint of the Jains). I shall always remember one Buddha in particular for the remarkably calm and sweet expression on his face. We lingered as long as possible, even viewing some of the last caves by lantern light; and left finally, feeling that we still had not seen anywhere near enough of this extraordinary human achievement.

We had dinner and stayed the night at the guesthouse in Aurangabad, a sort of hotel maintained by the government for the benefit of the people who visit the caves. By eight-thirty the next morning we were up and on our way to Ajanta. Here there is another series of caves in the shape of a horseshoe, dug out of the rock by Buddhist monks during the fourth, fifth and sixth centuries. For hundreds of years thereafter the existence of these caves was unknown, and they were only discovered in the early nineteenth century when some British soldiers were on maneuver. Since then excavation has been carried on steadily, first by the British and now by the Indians themselves, and an attempt is being made to preserve and restore everything they can. We were fortunate in being accompanied by the director of the work, who showed us as much as it was possible to see in one morning. The Ajanta Caves are especially known for their frescoes of figures and landscapes executed with great delicacy and amazing detail and in color that is almost beyond belief. There are scenes depicting the life of Buddha, the conquest of Ceylon; there are elephants and ships and dancing girls and princesses and singers. In some places only a patch of color remains, a fragment of a figure—a head or part of a gown; in other places whole scenes are almost complete. Here, as at Ellora, as you study the stupendous excavations from solid rock, the beauty of the carvings and frescoes, and then think of the tools that were available to these early artist-monks, you marvel at the infinite patience and industry and at the devotion that achieved such testimony to the glory of their God.

I was in fact so impressed by what I had seen that the following day, though we had to go on to Agra, I rose early enough to make another quick visit to the Ellora Caves, where in the early morning light I saw much that I had missed before. Their effect on me was, I think, even more overwhelming than it had been on first sight.

We arrived in Agra early enough in the afternoon to drive out to an interesting, old sixteenth-century fort that was built by Akbar, the grandson of Baber, the Asian prince who established the first Moslem dynasty in India. Akbar was probably the best and the wisest of Mogul emperors, a daring and resourceful general who conquered large parts of India, a tolerant and humane ruler who had the trust of both Moslems and Hindus, and as nearly as possible in that day unified the country. His courts at Agra and Delhi were centers of learning, where musicians, writers and artists of all sorts congregated. He was also the grandfather of Shah Jehan, who came to power about the time Louis XIV was king of France and the Massachusetts Bay Company was being established in America. And it was Shah Jehan who built the Taj Mahal.

I must own that by the time we got to Agra I was beginning to feel we had seen a great many forts and palaces and temples and mosques. I realized that I was no longer viewing them with the same freshness of interest and appreciation that I had felt during the early part of my visit. I think the others felt much the same way, which may have been one reason why we had all been talking more and more about the fact that no letters from home were reaching us. I had even cabled for news of my family. Therefore when we got back to Government House after our visit to Akbar's fort, though we knew we should leave immediately to get our first glimpse of the Taj Mahal at sunset, we all pounced on the letters we found waiting for us, and could not tear ourselves away until the last one had been read. Then, to our dismay, we found we had delayed too long; by the time we got to the Taj—about six-thirty—the light was beginning to fade.

What I have just said about feeling jaded cannot apply to the Taj. As we came through the entrance gallery into the walled garden and looked down the long series of oblong pools in which the Taj and the dark cypresses are reflected, I held my breath, unable to speak in the face of so much beauty. The white marble walls, inlaid with semiprecious stones, seemed to take on a mauve tinge with the coming night, and about halfway along I asked to be allowed to sit down on one of the stone benches and just look at it. The others walked on around, but I felt that this first time I wanted to drink in its beauty from a distance.

One does not want to talk and one cannot glibly say this is a beautiful thing, but one's silence, I think, says this is a beauty that enters the soul. With its minarets rising at each corner, its dome and tapering spire, it creates a sense of airy, almost floating lightness; looking at it, I decided I had never known what perfect proportions were before.

Everyone, I imagine, knows the story of the Taj: how Shah Jehan, who raised many beautiful palaces and tombs and mosques, built this, the most perfect of all, as a tomb for his lovely Persian wife, Mumtaz Mahal, so that in keeping with the promise he had made her, her name might be known forever. It is said he hoped sometime to build a tomb for himself of black marble on the other side of the river, to be connected to the Taj Mahal by a bridge. Before this dream was ever realized, however, he was deposed by his youngest son, Aurangzeb, and imprisoned in a wing of the palace. During his last days, so the story goes, he had his bed carried out to one of the courts from where he could look across at the tomb of the beautiful Mumtaz.

The white marble of the Taj symbolizes the purity of real love; and somehow love and beauty seem close together in this creation.

We returned in the evening to see it in the full moonlight, as everyone says you should, and though each time I saw it it was breath-taking, perhaps it was most beautiful by moonlight. We could hardly force ourselves to leave, and looked at it from every side, unable to make up our minds which was the most beautiful. I think though I liked my view from the bench halfway down the reflecting pools, possibly because water is so precious in India that it enhances everything.

Early the next morning—at seven-thirty to be exact—we visited the Taj again to see it in the clear daylight. It was still impressive and overwhelmingly lovely, but in a different way; and the marble looked slightly pinkish, as though it was being warmed by the sun.

As long as I live I shall carry in my mind the beauty of the Taj, and at last I know why my father felt it was the one unforgettable thing he had seen in India. He always said it was the one thing he wanted us to see together.

VIII

Our interlude of private sight-seeing over, we went on to Jaipur, which is now the capital of Rajasthan, an immense state in northern India formed by the union of the former princely Rajput states. In the age scale of India's cities, Jaipur is fairly modern, for it was founded in the eighteenth century by Jai Singh who made it the capital of his state. This was about the time the great Mogul empire was beginning to fall apart, following the death of Aurangzeb, and India was entering some dark years. But Jai Singh was a remarkable ruler: as a statesman he managed to keep his territory intact; as a mathematician, scientist and astronomer he was familiar with the latest Western developments in his fields and established a number of fine observatories. As a city planner he combined both taste and wisdom. The city of Jaipur, which he designed, is surrounded by a high, crenelated wall; its wide regular streets are laid out in a kind of gridiron pattern, and all the buildings are painted pink, sometimes with ornamentation in white. It is really a delightful city, with a pleasant residential district and a lovely palace whose grounds must cover fully a seventh of the city area. The present Maharajah, who now governs all Rajasthan as its Rajpramukh, is a progressive, well-traveled and highly Westernized young man who keeps very busy with his government duties. Holi, a harvest festival, was still being celebrated when we were there, and the Maharajah's clothes and skin, like those of everyone else we saw, were thoroughly stained with many colors. He told us they would simply have to wear off, for they could not be washed away.

Mr. Atal, our Foreign Office guide, who seemed to have relatives in many parts of India, told us that his father lived in Jaipur and that his little boy was with him, attending school. His wife we were to meet later in Allahabad, where she was visiting her mother.

Mr. Atal's father, we discovered, had a charming house with many rooms, courts, and running water and above all a wonderful rose garden. He makes a specialty of importing roses from all over the world, and was importing some for the gardens of Government House, which we saw later and which are really spectacular.

Our Mr. Atal was trained in the Indian Civil Service under the British; he was thoroughly familiar with Western customs and Western ways of thinking, but he also had a deep knowledge of his own country and his own people. It was a combination that made him an excellent escort for our trip and I felt very fortunate in having him with us. The day we were in Jaipur he was as excited as any young father might be to see his small son, and kept him with us as much as he could during our brief visit.

The boy and his father had an accident the morning we were there when their car was run into by a truck at a cross street. It might easily have proved very serious, but for a wonder neither was badly hurt, though both were shaken up and suffered a considerable shock and reaction. However, when they first told us about it, they made it sound as though nothing important at all had happened.

We stayed with the Maharajah and his very charming wife at Government House; and in the late afternoon drove out about five miles to see the fine old palace in the deserted city of Amber, which had been the capital before Jaipur was built. Now, they told us, it is inhabited only by snakes and tigers.

We had in Jaipur our only chance to ride on an elephant. Miss Corr and Dr. Gurewitsch took it, and said it was quite comfortable, but felt rather strange to move so slowly and majestically high up in the air above everyone else. I have been annoyed with myself ever since that I let myself be kept from trying it.

In the days when the Indian principalities were more or less independent, the prince of Jaipur used to hold magnificent parades three times a year for the people. On these occasions the elephants and horses and camels were decked out in unbelievably gorgeous trappings, so elaborate and so heavily ornamented that it took, I believe they said, ten men to carry the caparison that went on an elephant under the howdah or seat in which one rides. To my delight they brought out all this equipment and put it on the animals so we could see how they had looked in the parades. I must say it is a pity that it is no longer used.

The last day we were there it was suggested, among the possible choices, that we go out to see an old temple in the woods near the city, inhabited by swarms and swarms of monkeys who are attracted to it by the food they are given by visitors. It was always difficult when we were given alternatives, but I was glad we elected to see the monkeys. Though they infest India, we had not so far happened to see them in great numbers, and I found them extremely amusing. Some of them behaved like naughty children and their mothers cuffed them with resounding whacks which would not have been approved of in modern education but which seemed acceptable and decisive in the monkey world.

We were back at Government House in time for lunch, after stopping for a moment to see a school for poor children in which the Maharani was interested. Luncheon was served in a charming summer house on a lawn surrounded by high hedges. At the end of the garden a big tree shaded an extremely modern California outdoor grill, which they had recently imported from Hollywood. The Maharani was distressed because it did not work well, so I tried to look professional as I examined it, but it was so much more elaborate than anything I have at home I could only tell her that she would have to have a Californian explain it to her.

IX

Immediately after lunch in Jaipur we took off for New Delhi, this time to stay at Government House with President Prasad. A gentle and quiet man, but with great strength of character, Rajendra Prasad is deeply respected in India for his long years of loyal service to the country. He had been one of the outstanding leaders of the Congress Party and close to Gandhi during the bitter struggle for freedom; now, like the other leaders with whom he shares the responsibility for shaping India's future, he is imbued with a sense of India's importance and a feeling of urgency that drives him to work much harder and longer than he knows is wise. We all had tea with him in the afternoon and a pleasant, quiet talk in which he drew me out about my trip and told me something of his own problems.

In the evening Ambassador and Mrs. Bowles called for us and we all went to the opening of *The River*, a wonderful picture of India which I had seen previously in New York City. I was interested to observe that beautiful as it was, it seemed to have less of an impact on this Indian audience than on the audience in New York. The fact that the story dealt largely with English people in India, and that the scenes and background that were exotic and strange to New Yorkers were daily familiar to these Indians would, I expect, explain the difference in reaction.

On March 14, Mr. Atal and Madame Pandit went with me by train to Aligarh, a city in Uttar Pradesh (formerly the United Provinces) where I was to receive a degree from Aligarh Moslem University. Its chancellor is Dr. Zakir Hussain, a dignified and noble scholar who was opposed to the partitioning of India. Refusing to flee to Pakistan at the time of the riots, he rallied around him a good many other Moslems (there are, of course, millions of Moslems still living in India today) and was given the protection of both Gandhi and Nehru. All Hindus are grateful for his firm stand and his faith in them.

Our return trip was made by car, so that we might be back in the city in time to keep some afternoon engagements. For this trip Madame Pandit, who perhaps had learned in the United States what a picnic really is, had packed a delicious lunch of a variety of sandwiches, fruit and little cakes. We found a little government guesthouse by the side of a canal and drove in there to eat. It was delightful there by the running water; we needed no service, and everyone was relaxed and happy. As usual, however, we were conscious of the swift passage of time, so we could not linger, for I was determined to be back by three o'clock. One of the greatest problems on a crowded trip of this kind is to find time to do such simple things as getting one's hair washed. Mine was so filled with the dust of all our travels that it was practically stiff. My three o'clock appointment was for a shampoo, and I felt if I missed this one opportunity I would start out again and never have another chance.

Like a lot of other people, I imagine, I always have difficulty too in finding something in my travels to bring home to the little boys in the family. I thought on this trip that I was never going to find anything that would amuse my grandsons, but fortunately on a shopping expedition in New Delhi I saw some snake charmers' flutes spread out under the trees along the pavement and decided these might prove of interest to all the children.

One of the last things I did in New Delhi was to attend a reception given by the Nizam of Hyderabad, whom I had not met when I was there though I had seen him flying past in his automobile on his way to late afternoon prayers. This was his first visit to New Delhi since the new government of India was established. The British had left the native princes practically untouched in their powers, and had interfered very little in their administration of their states; and the Nizam resented the change in his position and the curtailment of his absolute power that had come with the new order of things. He had shown his resentment

[177]

by previously refusing to come to New Delhi for the regular meetings of state governors and rajpramukhs.

He is a short, slight man, not at all impressive looking, and he wears a tall, tight cap to increase his height. All kinds of stories had been circulating about how many planes it had required to move his retinue and how many wives and children he had brought with him. There was even a rumor that he did not know how many children he had. At the party, a very lavish affair despite his reputation for cautious spending, I met two of his daughters, both of whom were very quiet and subdued. He himself seemed pleasant, but I had no opportunity really to talk to him.

Our final day in New Delhi I had a long chat with Prime Minister Nehru, who wanted to know all about where I had been, the drives I had taken, what I had seen and the people I had met. He was, I thought, particularly pleased that I had enjoyed the Taj so much and had appreciated the Ellora Caves.

Afterward we went to the garden party given by President Prasad. It was quite a formal affair, attended by the entire diplomatic corps. As I moved down the path with the President, stopping at a certain spot to stand at attention while both national anthems were played, I felt queerly as though history were moving backward and we were going through a formal White House ceremony.

We had an opportunity that evening for a talk with Dr. Frank Graham, who was again negotiating with Pakistan

[178]

and India over Kashmir. Of course he could tell us nothing—and unhappily the dispute still stands about where it did that evening—but he is such a wonderful person that just to be with him always gives me confidence that something good is going forward. I think that everyone who comes in contact with him feels better simply for being in his presence. We talked happily about old days at Chapel Hill, and what the Senate was likely to do about more aid for India; and then I discovered that Dr. Graham, in all his visits to India, had never seen the Taj Mahal. I was horrified, and told him he should certainly not leave India this time without giving himself the pleasure of seeing one of the most beautiful things in the world.

I was really sorry to leave New Delhi. I had grown to feel at home there, and both at Government House and at the Prime Minister's everyone had been so kind that I had a pleasant sense of constant care and attention.

x

It was at this time that I made the trip to Etawah with Governor Modi, which I have described earlier. At the end of my day there I joined Madame Pandit in Allahabad, where I was going to be given a degree by the university.

Allahabad is the home of Prime Minister Nehru; and it is from this district that Madame Pandit is elected to Parliament. She had gone on ahead to open the house so we could stay there, and one of the Cabinet members, Dr.

Katju, the Home Minister, came up to be with us and show us around while we were there.

I was impressed by the house, which was large and old-fashioned, and both within and without declared the simple tastes of its owners. I had the Prime Minister's room and his study, and we were also given the use of the upstairs library. Here books from every corner of the world told of his avid and varied taste in reading. One evening after sitting up rather late in the library I almost fell over two prostrate figures lying on the veranda—either servants or guards, who had wrapped themselves completely in their white outer garments and were sleeping with apparent comfort on the bare wooden floor. Madame Pandit told me that she herself slept outside under the stars at night. The Prime Minister's bed was comfortable, but I could not help being aware that he scorned the soft modern bed with inner springs.

Dr. Katju proved himself a fascinating guide. I remember as one of my most delightful experiences the morning he took us out in a boat to the place where the sacred Ganges and the Jumna meet and mix their waters, and we made the traditional offering of milk. Here, for so many centuries that the beginning of the custom is lost in antiquity, hundreds of thousands of pilgrims have come every year at the time of the great bathing festivals, or *melas*, to wash away their sins in the holy water of the Ganges, and to make offerings in the temples. As we stepped from the car to get into the boat, we were greeted by some of the people whose families have lived thereabouts for generations and whose lives were wholly dedicated to caring for the needs of the pilgrims. The shore is dotted with huts, each bearing a flag denoting the particular god served by the holy man within.

Later in the morning we visited a prison where Nehru and his father and many other Indian leaders were confined by the British during one of the numerous sentences they incurred and indeed sometimes invited in the long passive resistance campaign that led to India's freedom. I often felt, talking to some of these people, that today they wear their prison sentences as other people wear medals of distinction.

Sometimes they were in solitary confinement for months; now and then one or two of them were in adjoining cells, where they would have a small place to cook, and one of the other prisoners would come in and prepare their meals. Washing facilities were outside the cells, and of the most primitive kind. The light was bad, but at night they were allowed to have a lantern. The only furniture was a cot and a stool, so life was fairly austere. However, letters, newspapers and books were usually allowed to the political prisoners, which must have helped to make the days of inactivity more tolerable.

I have a theory that their years of political imprisonment had a definite effect upon these men, many of whom now hold important government positions. They had much time for meditation and writing, and they learned to disassociate themselves from their surroundings and to think abstractly. In my first contact with the Prime Minister I was impressed by the feeling, which occasionally I also had even in large public gatherings, that he had withdrawn from his surroundings and, as far as his mind went, was hundreds of miles—or years—away. And indeed, in his fine *The Discovery of India*, written while he was imprisoned in Ahmadnagar Fort during the last war, Nehru says:

Time seems to change its nature in prison. The present hardly exists, for there is an absence of feeling and sensation which might separate it from the dead past. . . . The outer objective time ceases to be, the inner and subjective sense remains, but at a lower level, except when thought pulls it out of the present and experiences a kind of reality in the past or in the future. We live, as Auguste Comte said, dead men's lives, encased in our pasts, but this is especially so in prison where we try to find some sustenance for our starved and locked-up emotions in memory of the past or fancies of the future.

. . . so I made voyages of discovery into the past, ever seeking a clue in it, if any such existed, to the understanding of the present. The domination of the present never left me even when I lost myself in musings of past events and of persons far away and long ago, forgetting where or what I was. If I felt occasionally that I belonged to the past, I felt also that the whole of the past belonged to me in the present. . . .

I was glad Dr. Katju showed us the prison. Seeing it, I realized what India's leaders had willingly endured, and I felt I had a better understanding of the fire that burns in so many of them.

So far our visit to Allahabad had been full of interest and very peaceful. There remained only the convocation at the university at which I was to receive a degree, and the address to the student body that the students' council had asked me to deliver afterward. But at noon on that day, a number of the student organizations suddenly issued

An Open Letter to Mrs. Eleanor Roosevelt
on the Occasion of
Her Visit to the Allahabad University

Dear Madame:

We have known you as the wife of the late President Roosevelt of the United States of America under whose eminent leadership America fought shoulder to shoulder with the entire progressive humanity, against the dangers of Fascism. It would have been a matter of great joy to us, therefore, to welcome you in our midst had you come to our country as a private citizen in order to increase the good will and cultural ties between the peoples of the two countries, for who does not stand for the friendship among the nations.

Unfortunately, however, your recent statements at public gatherings testify to the contrary. Instead of bringing us a message of good will on behalf of the American people you have chosen to intervene in affairs which are our own domestic concern. For instance, while speaking at a reception given in your honor in New Delhi, you suggested that "Communism is fought with guns but with bread too." This appears to fit in with the imperialist scheme of using bread as a weapon of interference in internal politics of other countries. All patriots will resent it and regard it as derogatory to our national prestige. There are various shades of political opinion in our country which is evident from the picture that has emerged after the general elections. Any suggestion, particularly from a foreigner, however indirect, of using guns against any section is simply intolerable.

Quite recently a number of cultural delegations from abroad as well as renowned foreign personalities have visited our country. The Chinese Cultural Mission, the renowned French Physicists, Professor Joliot Curie and Madame Irene Curie, the distinguished Chilean poet, Pablo Neruda, the well-known Cambridge economist, Mr. Maurice Dobb and many others have come to our land but none of them chose to interfere in our internal politics and none of them found it necessary to slander and vilify this or that trend in the body-politic of our land. Indian delegations have also gone abroad but none of them made a bid for political guidance of the home country.

Representatives of American imperialism seem to have made a hobby of indulging in slander and abuse of personalities and ideologies they do not like. Even so responsible a person as the American Ambassador, Mr. Chester Bowles, the other day referred to Dr. J. C. Kumrappa, well-known Gandhian economist, as "a very foolish man" when he was asked to comment on the latter's view that "American aid is a noose around India's neck." Such is the disregard even for elementary courtesy by the highest representative of the Wall Street.

We are strongly of the opinion that Indian people alone are competent to decide the way of life they wish to lead and they will under no circumstances tolerate the arrogance of any foreigner to teach us what is good and bad, appropriate or inappropriate for us as a nation to do. This is a matter of choice exclusively for the Indian people to make. That we will brook no foreign interference from any quarter and in any shape is amply clear.

The letter contains, as you see, many of the usual allegations which one finds in Communist propaganda, and practically demands explanations. When Madame Pandit brought the letter to me, I was quite prepared to answer it and I suggested she let me handle it in the students' meeting. However, she was greatly worried. Someone had telephoned to the Prime Minister who, in reply, had said that if any discourtesy was shown to a guest of the government the university would be held responsible.

The newly elected head of the university and the registrar were deeply disturbed. They did not see how they could control the students; they felt that the students would ask embarrassing questions and perhaps interrupt my speech, and might even try to make trouble. Consequently, when Madame Pandit asked them whether they did not think it would be better if I stayed away from the student meeting, they promptly fell in with her suggestion that instead I see a representative group of about one hundred students on the lawn of her home.

I suggested that they forget that I was a guest of the government of India and let me go alone to the meeting and handle it as I would handle a meeting of young people at home, allowing them to ask questions and interrupt if they wished, and answering honestly. They all protested that that was impossible. Finally I said that since the letter was signed by about ten students, heads of the student organization, I would like to invite those ten to come and talk the letter over before meeting the others on the lawn. They agreed to this and I wrote the invitation, which was delivered at once.

We all went to the Convocation and I received my degree and made a brief acknowledgment. There was no disturbance, and immediately afterward I returned with Madame Pandit to the Prime Minister's house.

In the meantime word had reached the head of the student organization that I would not attend their meeting. They sent representatives to talk this over with Madame Pandit. She discovered that the vice-president of the main student organization, who was among this group, was also one of the signers of the Open Letter, and she asked him if he agreed with the statements it contained. He assured her that he did, and this so incensed her that she told him in that case his presence as a guest was not welcome in her home. He left and, of course, reported what she had said to the head of the organization and the other students. They now gathered outside the gates of the house some three thousand strong, with a loud speaker, and demanded that Madame Pandit come out and apologize for having ejected one of their members.

Meanwhile three of the students who had signed the open letter had accepted my invitation and were sitting

with me in a small study, discussing the leaflet. I answered
every point they made in it to the best of my ability and
with perfect candor, and I think they were convinced that
I was honest even though they may not have agreed with
me.

Finally I could no longer ignore the noise outside and
said that I thought I had better go and talk to the students.
The three who were with me told me that would do no
good, because they were not asking for me but for Madame
Pandit, who had insulted one of their members. Nevertheless, as time went on and our conversation came to an end
I decided that this could not be permitted to drag out
indefinitely, so I went to the gate where I found the poor
registrar standing on a chair, trying to induce the students to
return to the university. I took his place on the chair and
talked to them for ten minutes, at the end of which time
the president of the organization, standing in the middle of
the crowd, announced that they did not like to receive their
guests across a gate and would be extremely grateful if I
would come to the students' hall even for a short time. I
agreed to this if they would go back immediately and allow
me to join them there. This seemed to meet with their
approval and they started to move away. I turned to the
president and the registrar and said they could go with me
but we must take no one else. Someone suggested an un-
obtrusive guard, but I said no: no police and no soldiers
were to go with us either. They accepted this stipulation

and we drove off in the car, leaving Dr. Gurewitsch looking rather unhappy about the whole idea.

When we arrived at the students' hall it was jammed. They took me up to the platform and presented me with a written and framed address of welcome and invited me to respond. I spoke for a short time in a general vein on democracy and human rights; then I thanked them and was warmly applauded and allowed to leave without the slightest demonstration and with a perfectly amicable spirit existing on both sides.

The list of questions prepared for me by the students at Allahabad is, I think, not without interest:

(1) What is an un-American activity? Why is there ruthless suppression of so-called un-American activities?

(2) Do you propose to visit the real India, which according to Mahatma Gandhi lies in its seven million villages, and informally contact the villagers?

(3) Is it one of your objects of your visit to India to see the labor slums, particularly in Bombay, Calcutta, Ahmadabad, Delhi and Cawnpore?

(4) Why do Americans hesitate to pour their capital into India when full facilities are assured them?

(5) Why is America so concerned to check communism in Asia when President Truman agrees that Russia and the U.S.A. can exist side by side?

(6) Do you think that democracy in the real sense of

the term can never be realized until and unless the principle of self-determination of the nations is given full effect both in letter and spirit?

(7) Is it not a fact that the neutrality and territorial independence of the smaller nations owing to the technique of modern warfare are rendered a farce as such nations have to depend for their defense on big powers?

(8) How do you justify the uncommon and keen interest evinced by the U.S.A. in Asia at present? Is it really characterized by purely humanitarian consideration?

(9) Why in the land of Lincoln and Roosevelt is there still discrimination, color prejudice and Negro lynching?

(10) Is it a fact that nearly thirteen million persons are unemployed in the United States? If so why should this be? (wholly or partially)

(11) What is the role of the students in American life?

(12) What do you think of "third force" in International politics? Don't you think it is in the best interest of India to keep aloof from both the warring blocs?

(13) How are you liking India and what impressions are you carrying back with you?

(14) What is your personal view about the admission of the People's Government of China into the UNO?

(15) What role has the works of Swami Vivekananda

played in the life of the American people? What are your views, therefore, about the Indian way of life as enunciated in the Vedantic philosophy?

(16) What is the lot of Communists in America?

To the fifteenth question I had to plead ignorant. Most of the others I tried to answer in my press conferences and in my talks with the students at various universities.

I was not surprised to find, in talking to university groups, that the questions they asked me were reminiscent of those that young people in the United States used to ask me during the 1930's. The young Indians live under different circumstances, they have a different background, but in seeking a solution to their problems they react much as our young people did when they were searching for an answer to what they felt was the failure of democracy to meet their needs during the years of the great depression. The surprising thing to me is not that there should be frustration among the youth of India, when there is so much that needs to be done and they are so ill-equipped with the skills to do it, but that there is not more unrest. The young people of India will probably straighten out as soon as there are jobs for them to work at and they have been given the training to fill them.

Prime Minister Nehru has always felt apparently that the Hindu religion, with its emphasis on nonviolence and truth, was inherently incompatible with communism, and that there was therefore no danger that communism would ever gain a real foothold in India. The rise in the Communist vote in India's first election—they won 5.5 per cent of the elected seats in Parliament—seems to have been a shock to many government leaders. Their strength was chiefly in the south of India, where they capitalized on the acute food shortage, and where, perhaps significantly, the literacy rate is highest.

Nevertheless, it was not in the south, but in Allahabad, that I encountered the most open demonstration of Communist influence on the students. Happily, none of the other degrees I received carried with them the same experience.

I was very fortunate in the number of universities that were kind enough to honor me. For, in addition to the two I have already mentioned, I was given a degree by New Delhi University, whose chancellor is President Prasad, and by Santiniketan, which was founded by Rabindranath Tagore. His son is now the head of it. I particularly liked my degree from this university. It is in Sanskrit and was inscribed on a copper plate by a young Turkish student. I also liked the lovely silk scarf they give with it instead of a hood.

After the commencement exercises I went back to the president's house for lunch. I have always admired Tagore's poetry, but I had not realized until I saw the library of his works what a prolific writer he had been; nor had I realized until I saw his paintings and sketches on the walls that he was an artist as well as a poet.

Tagore was an intimate friend of Gandhi, whose principles are a part of the university's creed. The ideal of service is emphasized particularly, and many of the students spend their vacations working in the villages or city slums. One of the four young Americans who are studying there has become, outwardly at least, almost an Indian, even wearing the seamless garment of khadi, or homespun, that Gandhi urged all Indians to spin and wear.

I had a question and answer period with the students in the afternoon, and came away with the feeling that they were to some extent divorced from the real world. I do not mean that they were unaware of what was happening in the world, for they were not; but they seemed to stand apart from it, and lived almost as if in an ivory tower. I am sure the young Americans who are studying there are getting an excellent classical education; but if education in its broadest sense should prepare one to live in one's own world, I wonder if they won't find it difficult to adapt themselves when they emerge from the environment of this university, where the stress is wholly on the intellectual, artistic and spiritual life?

XI

One of the things we of the West who are attempting to understand India must realize is why the Communist philosophy is perhaps easier for them to accept than our own.

It is a fact that very few of them know what we are talking about when we speak of freedom in the abstract, as we are accustomed to in the United States or Great Britain or other

European countries. They have had no experience with the
reality; for they have hardly ever been free. It is only in the
last six years that they have had their own government; and
they held their first election only a year and a half ago. The
great majority of them have been hungry all their lives;
indeed, they have been hungry for generations, and they will
become hungrier as their population increases, unless drastic
measures are taken.

But their poverty has been made more bearable by their
religion which teaches the worthlessness of material possessions and the virtue of voluntary renunciation, and promises
to the upright the reward of a better life in the next incarna-
tion. For it is part of the Hindu belief that when a person
dies he is reborn again in some other form; and whether
that form is higher or lower in the scale of existence depends
upon his conduct in his present life.

In effect, what it means to a starving Hindu peasant in
Madras, to a Hindu dweller in the slums of Bombay, to a
Hindu refugee sleeping in the streets of Calcutta is that
since he cannot eat and must go without, he can at least go
without voluntarily and patiently, and thereby store up
treasures for the life to come.

So they have gone on, these masses of people, living closely
together, suffering together and sharing a deep sense of
brotherhood and a common reverence for those who are
willing to renounce the good things of the world and to join
with their brothers in suffering. It is not unusual for a prince,

when he feels he is approaching his last years, to give away all he has and retire to a mountain top or a cave, placing his begging bowl where the poor can put in it their offerings of food from their meager stock, knowing that having become a holy man he can repay them by prayer. Holy men with their begging bowls are fairly common sights in India.

The appeal renunciation has for the Indian people was borne out by something told me by Dr. Katju, the cultured and charming Cabinet minister who showed us about Allahabad. The morning we went out on the river I asked him about the significance of the different emblems on the flags that floated above the huts and tents of the holy men along the banks. He explained to me that Hindus believe in the existence of one Supreme God, Brahma, who however has various aspects and who manifests himself in various ways. These different aspects have been personified in a number of lesser gods, who are represented by images. Each family has its own particular household god, whom it worships, but all these gods are simply different manifestations or expressions of the one Universal God. Then he told me a story of Krishna, the warrior hero who is worshiped as the human embodiment of the great god Vishnu the Preserver. Vishnu, Brahma the Creator and Shiva the Destroyer are the three principal gods of the Hindu trinity. In a way, the tale is reminiscent of some of the old Greek myths. Krishna left his wife for a journey to far away places and was gone many years. After he left she bore him a son of whose coming Krishna knew nothing; and she brought the boy up to guard the house and to let no one enter it. One day, without notice, Krishna returned. His son barred the entrance and Krishna, incensed, cut off the boy's head. Finding his wife within, he demanded to know who it was that had dared to deny him entrance, and whose head he had cut off. His wife in horror told him that it was his own son. Grief-stricken, and desiring to make amends, Krishna killed and cut off the head of an elephant which he brought back and put on his son. To this day Ganesh—the god with the elephant's head—is the defender of all homes; and all over India you see his image on little plaques fastened over or near the doors of the houses.

Dr. Katju finally turned to me and said: "Those flags are there to guide the pilgrims, so each of them will know where to find the holy man who represents his special household god." Then he added, rather sadly, I thought: "You know, Mrs. Roosevelt, if I were to give up my position in the Cabinet and give away everything I have made in my life and sit with a begging bowl under one of those flags, I would have one hundred times more influence with the people than I have today."

I thought then of Gandhi who gave up his considerable income as a lawyer and everything he had and chose instead the simple and austere life of an ashram. The people loved him for his sacrifice and renunciation; it was, largely, the secret of his enormous influence with them and was what made it possible for him to become a national leader.

In my mind's eye I saw a picture of the home for Untouchable boys that Gandhi had founded on the outskirts of New Delhi and of the bare little room on the second floor that he used when he went there to stay with them. I saw the room when we were in New Delhi, and I stood at the entrance awed by the thought of the power of the man who had lived there. All there ever was in that room is still there—a rug, a rolled-up pad that was used at night as a bed, a pillow. People who came to see him sat cross-legged on the floor before him, as I should certainly have had to do had I ever had the good fortune to be received by him. I suppose if you have done it from birth, squatting on your heels is very comfortable and you can do it even in your old age. I myself find it practically impossible, and it irritates me that I have let my knees grow stiff.

We in the West do not demand or expect such austerity and self-denial in the lives of our public men, and though we might respect them for it, it would not greatly enhance their influence. But the hungry people of India were won by Gandhi's life of voluntary renunciation and service, and they followed him as long as he lived.

The philosophy of renunciation, combined with appalling poverty, has created a situation made to order for the Communists, who have shaped their propaganda cleverly. They do not promise fantastic material rewards; they say something like this—"Your lives have been difficult. You have known only hardship and poverty. If you will surrender your will to the state, which labors for the good of the people as a whole, the state will see that all of you have work to do for which you are compensated; and all of you will have something to eat. It may not be as much as you would like, but you will be assured of enough to keep body and soul together. And you will have the satisfaction of knowing that throughout the Communist world all your brothers will share equally with you, and are also enjoying the fruits of their own labor."

Freedom to eat is one of the most important freedoms; and it is what the Communists are promising the people of India.

Our Western doctrines are less easy to grasp. We strive for great prosperity; we want to be free to progress as far and as rapidly as we can, and we have enough confidence in ourselves not to want to be restricted to a minimum. Our laws may set certain minimum standards, but none of us wants to be kept by law from working for better things.

To the Indians, however, we seem to be interested in material gains only. Moreover what we offer, what we assure them is possible, is so far removed from anything within the experience—or even the knowledge—of most of them that it sounds, quite simply, fantastic, not believable. We cannot be sincere, they think. But what the Communists offer is entirely understandable. The possibilities they hold out have the advantage of being something the Indian people can imagine achieving; that they can see as not too far removed from the pattern of their past or from their vision and hope for the future. Yes, they say, this much possibly is within our reach. They have no background of knowledge that would enable them to detect the speciousness of the Communist promises; they do not realize that the Communist system is a brake not only on material but spiritual advance; they have not yet made the connection between freedom and not just less hungry stomachs but full stomachs.

There is no question in my mind that Prime Minister Nehru is trying to develop a democracy that, though perhaps not exactly like ours, will ensure all the people personal freedom. But if an accompanying material prosperity is also to be achieved—and the government will not be successful unless it can demonstrate certain progress on the material side—considerable education and re-education of the people will be necessary. For a belief in the virtue of renunciation is not an incentive to hard work for material gain; but only hard work by all the people is going to bring any real betterment of their living conditions. Somehow a spiritual incentive, a substitute for renunciation, will have to be found. Somehow they must be made to realize the living and exciting possibilities of the freedom and democracy their new government offers them.

These ideas had been gradually forming in my mind as I traveled about India, and in my last talk with Prime Minister Nehru the night before I left Calcutta, I tried to put them into words for him. I asked him first whether my feeling about the Indians' great admiration of renunciation was correct, and I told him what Dr. Katju had said. He was quick to answer that he thought the Indian people wanted their public men to do their work; but then he added: "They do admire renunciation," and from the tone of his voice I gathered that he admired it too.

I went on to ask whether there were not two separate lines that would have to be pursued before the goals of the Five Year Plan could be achieved. One was of course the line of material progress, involving the procurement of the material aid, technical assistance, supplies and machines needed to develop India's agricultural and industrial economy and trade. With, in the meantime, enough food grains to keep the people from starving. These things the technically advanced countries of the West could help with.

But the other requisite of success we could not help with —to discover an equivalent to renunciation. Only the Indian leaders, especially Nehru himself, with his deep understanding of the Indians' inner needs, could judge what spiritual incentives would induce them to make the effort necessary to obtain material satisfaction.

Our material wealth has come to us almost as a by-product of our effort to fulfill our spiritual and democratic ideals and as a result of our philosophy of work. But our ideals are peculiar to our culture; they satisfy us, but they would not necessarily satisfy the Indian people. As a Westerner, I could be told that I must work hard to attain material success for myself and my nation because the Lord did not intend people to die almost before they had lived; and did intend them to live and contribute to the general well-being of their world and to the development of their country. That is the way civilization advances, and India could contribute greatly to its advancement. These considerations are a sufficient moral and spiritual spur for us. "But would they be enough to make the Indian people work?" I asked Nehru.

My own feeling is that with their religious and cultural background something different will be required to spark in them the conviction that the modern struggle of a highly technologically developed state is worth while.

I do not know whether my analysis is right or whether I am simply imagining a situation; yet when I was talking to Nehru that night, he gave me no feeling that I was wrong.

I think it is well for all of us as we size up the effect of the Communist promises in this area of the world, and the possible success of our own conception of democracy, to bear in mind that our world and way of life is an unknown quantity to the people of the East. This is one of the hurdles we will have to get over before we can hope fully to understand each other.

When I was going through Los Angeles on my way home, Paul Hoffman asked me to lunch with him and his colleagues of the Ford Foundation. They had only recently made a rather more extensive trip than mine, and we exchanged impressions. When I told Mr. Hoffman of my last talk with Nehru, he said he had tried to say something to him of a similar nature. He told the Prime Minister that in our country the spark that fired the imagination of all young people was the Horatio Alger story, the story of the poor boy who always becomes a great success. The Prime Minister, he said, did not seem to understand. I do not know whether he understood what I was trying to tell him any better, though I put it a little differently, but the point I am making is that the Horatio Alger story and all its implications about the American way would, I am afraid, be totally unintelligible to most of the people of India.

Somehow they must be brought to realize that our desire for material success is coupled with spiritual motivations as well, and they must understand what these motivations are. This may mean that we shall first have to clarify them for ourselves. In the process, perhaps many of us will come to see that fundamentally our life is based on religious beliefs that in some ways are not unlike those of the Hindus. We believe in our God. Many of us in the West who are Christians believe that, through a mystery we cannot understand, Christ was the Son of God sent to this world to sacrifice His life to save us. The spirit of sacrifice is not so far removed from the renunciation of the Hindus, and it runs through the whole history of Christianity. Even those who do not accept Christ as a God think of Him as a great and good man with God-like qualities, and admire and love the willingness to sacrifice for others that He and His disciples taught and practiced.

An understanding of our own spiritual foundations may be one of the bridges we need to better understanding of the East and its people.

XII

In Allahabad we regretfully said good-by to our very kind hostess, Madame Pandit, for we would not be seeing her again the remainder of our trip. I can never be grateful enough to her for the thought she gave to the preparations for my visit and for the care and attention with which she watched over us while we were there.

My next recollections of India are of the old city of Benares, the holiest of all India's cities, where thousands of pilgrims come every year to worship in its shrines and to bathe in the Ganges. Not far outside the city is the Deer Park where Buddha is said to have preached his first sermon.

We were given an official welcome at the airport, but here we had asked to be allowed to stay with a friend of Dr. Gurewitsch—Mr. Burnier, the young Frenchman who is married to the charming dancer of *The River*, Radha Sri Ram.

On the way to his house we took a boat along the Ganges, passing the crowds of people on the ghats, the landing places with long flights of wide steps that line the bank and lead down to the river, and saw the smoke rising from the burning funeral pyres. When the river is high, they told me, it rises almost to the top of the steps, though as I looked at that long flight I found it difficult to believe.

The Ganges is a sacred river, for it was supposed to have
flowed from the brow of Lord Shiva, and all Hindus wish
when they die to have their ashes scattered on its water.

We left our boat finally and climbed the steps to mix
with the crowds and walk through some of the narrow
streets thronged with people and animals constantly passing
and going in and out of shops and temples. Narrow streets
have one value in this climate, however, for they shut out
the sun, and even in March it was very hot. The streets are
lined with innumerable open booths selling brasses, stone-
ware, embroideries, brocades of all sorts. Some of the more
pretentious merchants had their entrances on the street
and their shops on the second floor.

Mr. Burnier's house was charming. It was largely of brick
and was built around a courtyard, one room deep. The courtyard was filled with potted flowers, and the long living room
faced the Ganges. We went out on the balcony that over-
hung the river and looked down on what I suppose was a
typical Benares scene. There was a herd of buffalo bathing
in the water, with only their backs showing. Nearby at a
little wharf, two women sat dabbling their feet, while a small
girl of five or six bathed just below them. Suddenly the child
began to wail and the cries were heart-rending. We won-
dered why the women seemed so uninterested. Finally the
older woman girded up her sari and started to wade toward
the child, who was bobbing up and down in the water, coming up each time with a louder wail than before. Just as the
woman nearly reached her, the child came up holding a tiny

pair of pants. All was serene then, and she spread them
out on the stone to dry. The significance of this little drama,
I think, was that the child had no other garment, and to
lose one's only garment was a serious matter. At five or six,
the habit of renunciation hadn't taken a firm enough hold
to make her indifferent to her loss.

The only other city we visited in India was Calcutta,
which was our last stopping place. This is not a city that I
recommend as the first to be seen in India. Here the poverty
seems even more acute than elsewhere; the slums are appalling and there is a great deal of illness. Malaria and epilepsy
abound; elephantiasis is not rare; and every day the newspaper matter-of-factly lists the number of people who have
died from cholera, plague and smallpox.

Calcutta, which is on the Hooghly River, about eighty-
five miles from the Bay of Bengal, is the chief port of eastern
India, as well as one of its largest industrial centers,
and such cities are seldom clean or healthy. Conditions
have been made worse by the fact that thousands of refugees from Pakistan have poured in here, and despite
the heroic efforts of the government to get them under
shelter, many are still homeless. Walking in the streets after
dark one night, I nearly fell over a figure wrapped in his
garment sleeping on the edge of the sidewalk. Elsewhere
about the city I saw people sleeping on the front of monu-
ments, on the steps of buildings and under the protection
of the bridge arches, the sacred cows asleep on the sidewalk

beside them. Many a man, when he quits work at night, simply puts his pallet on the sidewalk in front of his shop and lies down. What it is like when it rains and he must sleep within the four walls of the cubbyhole where he works I cannot imagine, but I suppose the impossible becomes possible when shelter is essential.

One heartening note, however, is provided by the wonderful work being done by the various women's organizations of Calcutta. I attended one of their meetings at Government House, which was presided over by Lady Mitter, an Englishwoman, and was extremely impressed by the exhibits illustrating their work. They maintain nursery schools, run adult education classes, give instruction in sanitation and hygiene and child care, and start centers where the refugees and other poor people are taught various handicrafts.

The magnificent way the women have taken hold here illustrates as well as anything could the determination and spirit with which they are seizing their opportunities and accepting their responsibilities. All over India today you find women not only going into social work, but heading up girls' colleges and schools, and holding political office, both appointive and elective. Some women are successfully combining several jobs, like Mrs. Hansa Mehta, whom I was delighted to see in Bombay, and who is head of a school near Madras as well as India's delegate on the Human Rights Commission.

On my last full day in Calcutta I dined with Mr. and Mrs.

Wilson, our Consul General and his wife, and attended a meeting to celebrate the opening of the United States Information Service Center. These centers are stocked with books, pictures, posters, magazines and documentary films which give the Indian people an honest picture of American life and people, and a clearer understanding of our policies. India is working with our own USIS people here, helping to disseminate knowledge about the United States and interpreting the material to the people who come in. And they do come in. They come in from the streets in throngs —proof, I think, of how hungry they are for information. It is a great pity we cannot afford to establish these centers in all the cities that ask for them. It would not only help them to know us as we really are, but would help to offset the distorted picture of us presented by Russian propaganda, second-rate American movies, the insensitive and tactless behavior of some of the Americans who go to India and the boastfulness of some who merely stay at home. And make no mistake. The Russian propaganda in India is excellent. They have really beautiful posters depicting the Utopian conditions in the Soviet Union, and stock the bookshops with Russian books made to sell for a few pennies. The Indian press, with a few exceptions, is generally reluctant to publish anything very critical of the Soviet Union, since they feel it is important in the country's present state of development and preparedness to remain on as friendly terms as possible with such a close and powerful neighbor.

Consequently it is not easy for the Indian people to learn the unpleasant facts of Soviet life that lie behind the rosy propaganda, or to spot the falsity in the picture the Soviets give them of us—unless we help them to.

It was this last evening that I also had the long conversation with Nehru that I described earlier. He is a delightful and understanding person, and I have no words to express my admiration of his extraordinary courage, for the weight of the burden he carries is heavy.

6

Nepal

In between my visits to Benares and Calcutta, I made a quick trip by air to the tiny kingdom of Nepal, lying on the slopes of the Himalayas, between the northern border of India and the southern border of Tibet. It had not been planned as part of my itinerary, but in talking to Ambassador Bowles one day I mentioned that I was anxious to have a really good view of the high mountains of the Himalayas. He thought the way to do it was to fly into Katmandu in Nepal, and then fly along the whole range.

It is only recently that Nepal built an airport and that an air service was established between New Delhi and Katmandu, the capital. Katmandu lies in a fertile valley fifteen miles long surrounded by high mountains, and is not reached by the railroad. Up to three years ago one had to go by train across Pakistan and then for two days by horseback, donkey or foot over the mountains to Katmandu. The city and surrounding villages are served by a cable railway nineteen miles long, but most transportation is still by foot. The chassis of the few trucks one sees on the road had to be carried in over the mountains on the backs of porters; and the impressive Rolls-Royce in which we were driven around was brought in the same way. There are not many cars of any kind, however, for the roads are few and bad. I do not think I have ever felt so far out of the world.

We stayed in a palace which is at present occupied by Mr. and Mrs. Rose. Mr. Rose is the director of the Point Four program in Nepal, and Mrs. Rose explained to me that they either had to live in the palace or in a hovel with a dirt floor. There was nothing in between. They had been installed only ten days and were just getting accustomed to the peculiarities of their abode when we arrived. There was a bathroom, but all the water had to be carried up from the kitchen. There were a few other inconveniences in connection with this bathroom, but on the whole I thought we were lucky to be as comfortable as we were, and I was very grateful to the Roses for taking us in, particularly as they were hardly settled themselves.

The small daughter of the family took me on a tour of exploration in the early morning. We inspected first the empty rooms of the palace which the Roses hope to use as offices and quarters for other members of the staff when they arrive. Outside we saw the walled-in gardens and a quite wonderful stable and barn, now occupied, if I remember rightly, by just one goat. However, the promise of a pony was very present in the mind of my young guide.

At the luncheon reception given for me by Mr. and Mrs.

Rose I had a chance to talk to some of the young Nepalese students who were being sent to the United States to study agriculture (Nepal is almost wholly agricultural; handicrafts are about the only industry) and medicine. I began to inquire about the facilities for practicing medicine that would be available to the medical students on their return to Nepal and at first made little headway with my questions. After some time one of the foreign embassy people said to me in a low voice: "Nobody goes to the hospital here until they know they are going to die."

That conditions in the hospital should be so bad that nobody would go to it except as a last resort seemed to me shocking. I talked about it to the Prime Minister, and spoke of the need for bringing in new equipment to modernize the hospital and to provide the newly trained doctors on their return with the same kind of instruments that they would have become accustomed to using in the United States. The Prime Minister, who appeared to me a progressive and sensible human being, seemed to see my point, and I had a feeling he might try to procure the essential equipment.

Nepal, until fairly recently, had a rather unusual administrative system—a titular king, who was merely a figurehead and rarely seen, and a hereditary prime minister who exercised the real power and who was always succeeded by a member of his own family. The present king of Nepal—Maharajadhira Tribhubana Bir Bikram—who came to the

throne in 1911, was later exiled for a short period, and his
three-year-old grandson was installed in his place. However,
he came back to Nepal in 1951, put an end to rule by
hereditary premiers and established a popular constitutional
government.

We met the king, and his two official wives, when he
received us that evening prior to the buffet dinner he was
giving in my honor. He and his wives were very cordial; but
I cannot say conversation flowed easily between us, and I
was relieved when an aide announced it was time to go into
the hall where the dinner was being given.

The younger brother of the Prime Minister was also
at the dinner. He told me he was coming to the United
States soon. He was not only younger than his brother,
whom he has since displaced in office, but, I thought, less
stable and mature. I only hope the development of the
country will not be affected by the change of prime minis-
ters, for there is much to be done there.

The Nepalese seemed to me quiet, gentle and hard-work-
ing, people you could like but who would have little ability
to achieve the things they wanted by themselves. It will take
wise leadership and intelligent help from outside to prepare
them for living in a democracy.

The people seem to be of two stocks—the Mongols, who
so far as anyone knows were the original inhabitants, and
the descendants of the Aryans, who came in from India,
mixed with the Mongolic tribes and in the eighteenth cen-

tury became predominant. The official religion and that observed by the majority of the people is Hinduism, but there are also many Buddhists, particularly in the north. The morning after our arrival we visited a Buddhist temple in a village where the Chinese Lama lives. He was away, so we did not see him, but we walked about the village and saw a number of other temples and shrines. There are, I am told, over twenty-five hundred Buddhist temples in this valley. They are extremely ornate and lavishly decorated with skillful wood carving. But they were not, I thought, really beautiful.

Leaving Katmandu for Calcutta, we flew as close to the Himalayas as possible in order to obtain the best view of the mountains. Unfortunately it was cloudy a good part of the time, though we did have a glimpse of Mount Everest and of some of the other high peaks. Perhaps the clouds around the mountains really enhanced their height for they still looked overwhelmingly impressive and majestic.

7

Homeward Bound

I

My visit to India ended, I headed home with no real stops except for a few days in Indonesia. We touched down briefly in Rangoon and stayed overnight in Bangkok, where we were delightfully entertained by our Ambassador, Edwin Stanton, and his wife and by officials of the Siamese government. The next morning we were off again at seven for Djakarta, the capital of the Indonesian Republic, with only an hour and a half stop in Singapore.

It had been getting steadily hotter ever since we left India, the kind of damp hotness that we Westerners find difficult to take until we become acclimated. Indonesia lies along the equator, and by the time we landed at Djakarta, where Merle Cochrane, our Ambassador, met us, we were thoroughly uncomfortable.

Indonesia is principally an agricultural country. The three thousand islands in this archipelago grow a great variety of products—rice (there are rice paddies everywhere you look), nuts, palm trees, rubber trees (here on Java I saw my first rubber plantation), tobacco, coffee, tea, sugar. It is lush tropical country.

We dined with the President and Mrs. Soekarno, both friendly, kind people. Dr. Soekarno is Indonesia's first President, and a veteran in the fight for her independence. He is greatly interested in modern painters and has a young artist living with them who paints scenes of Indonesian life. After dinner he showed me his own excellent collection of modern paintings, which I thoroughly enjoyed.

Indonesia is one of the world's rich countries, not only agriculturally but in natural resources. She has vast supplies of tin, coal and oil, and ample mineral deposits. It seemed to me that here was a country that could support as great a development as she was prepared to undertake, and use, with perhaps phenomenal benefit to the living standards of the people, the economic and technical assistance the United Nations and the United States could give her. Yet only the month before my arrival the Cabinet had resigned over a disagreement about accepting help under our Mutual Security program. Later, to be sure, they did agree to accept some technical and economic aid, but rejected the military aid clause.

While I was there we talked over the difficulties the United States has had with Indonesia; and I came to the conclusion that it would perhaps be wise not to press our MSA program too fast on these people, particularly the military part of it. They are not antagonistic to us, but like other countries that have only recently become free, they are definitely wary of us. Indonesia does not want to risk becoming economically dependent; she does not welcome too much in the way of leadership and guidance from the outside.

Indonesia has come through a long period of guerrilla warfare and has gained her freedom. She has to settle down to organize her own government, to regulate her relationship with the Netherlands and the rest of the world, and she has some problems that are not easy to solve within her own domain. Right in Djakarta she has a large Chinese population. The government has recognized the Republic of China, so there is an active Communist center in the Chinese embassy there. It is very easy for Chinese Communists to infiltrate into Indonesia and it would be foolish to think they are not doing so. Therefore we would be unwise not to co-operate to the best of our ability in the development of Indonesia in order to make life more worth while for the people. But to expect that Indonesia is ready to enter into an alliance in which she accepts a certain percentage of military responsibility I think is asking too much and perhaps does us more harm than good. She is jealous of her independence; she should be allowed to formulate her own plans and programs. We should not insist where she does not signify her willingness to co-operate with us. In the long run, if we wait for the government of Indonesia to ask for our help, I think we will find ourselves further ahead than if we press her to accept our plans. Even though she may do so, it will be reluctantly done.

In Indonesia, as in many other places, we have both friends and enemies. Again it is deeds that will prove our real intentions.

Because Indonesia is a rich country, many business people are attracted to it. They, as well as our official government representatives, should be used to create good will, but they should be carefully briefed, and must walk with extreme tact and care.

II

Leaving Djakarta, we headed for the Philippines and the last speaking appointment of my trip. Both there and in Indonesia I felt guilty, because time compelled me to refuse so many of the engagements I was invited to fill.

As we flew in over the bay toward Manila, Bataan and the island of Corregidor were pointed out below. To any American those names will bring back a page in our history that we will long remember with deep regret and sorrow.

No sooner had we stepped off the plane and been greeted by Ambassador and Mrs. Spruance than I was confronted with a request for a press conference and an expression of my views on the Philippines, though I would have thought it obvious that I could have little to say at that point. I am afraid, since I was there only twenty-four hours, I have not much more to offer now.

However, during the evening, when I met the women who were to be my guides the following day, I learned how much they at least thought it was possible to pack into that time. The first thing the next morning, after laying wreaths on the graves of some of the Philippine martyrs of the war, I was taken to visit the old Spanish church of San Agustin, in whose vestry Admiral Dewey signed the treaty transferring ownership of the Philippines from Spain to the United States. This is the only building in the old walled city part of Manila that has been left standing by earthquakes, bombings and the desperate fighting that finally retook Manila from the Japanese. All of Manila still shows the terrible scars of the devastation wrought by the war; the New City was badly damaged, and the Old City completely erased—except for this church. The government has begun an extensive rebuilding program, with American aid, but here too, in this already crowded, war-torn city, bad conditions have been aggravated by a refugee problem. Over 150,000 refugees have fled into Manila to escape the Communist-led Huk guerrillas who make life unsafe in the outlying villages. So there are slums, overcrowding, not enough jobs.

After leaving the church, we went to a United Nations information center where people could learn about the various activities of the organization; and then to a tuberculosis sanitarium. Tuberculosis is one of their most serious health problems. Before the war, the United States had made remarkable gains in reducing the prevalence not only of tuberculosis but of malaria, beriberi and other diseases common in the East. During the war of course much of the headway that had been made was lost, and the Philippine government has had to attack the problem all over again.

Our next visit was to a children's village for orphans whose parents were killed in the war. Here too are the children of lepers; and though they are separated from the others, an effort is made to give them as normal a life as possible. Their parents are housed in the leper colony.

I had not realized before my visit that the Philippine women were playing such a positive role in the development of the country, so I was surprised at the extent of their activities. I was particularly impressed by the work being done by the rural schoolteachers, which, it seems to me, will eventually revolutionize village life in the Philippines. The plans now under way are to some extent based on the mass-education program that the American-educated scholar, James Yen, was directing in China before the arrival of the Communists obliged him to leave. The Philippines have free elementary education for both boys and girls, and the teachers are trying to bring it within the reach of more children; and they have begun fundamental education classes for older people who have not had a chance to learn to read and write (about half the population is literate). At the same time they are planning to teach improved farming techniques, and simple sanitation and health measures.

The morning ended up with a private audience with President Quirino. I had learned earlier that two of his daughters and his wife were killed by Japanese machine-gunners only a few days before the city was liberated. Our meeting was followed by a pleasant luncheon party at which another daughter, who is charming, acted as hostess. I was fascinated by the beautifully embroidered shirts worn by the men, and before I left Manila asked someone to buy some for my own menfolk—though I don't know whether they will ever wear them.

In the afternoon I spoke at Rizal Stadium to a considerable audience of government officials, diplomats, delegates of all the women's organizations and representatives from the other islands in the Philippines. The stadium, I learned, was named after one of the nineteenth-century leaders in the movement for independence, who was executed by the Spanish. It is such a big place that I had worried about making myself heard, and I had also been concerned about language difficulties. To my relief, everyone apparently was able to understand me, since, as I realized later, English is the medium of instruction, though Tagalog, a Malayan dialect, has been adopted as the national language.

After my speech, we all watched an exhibition of native dancing, which I thought was really outstanding—and by now I felt I had a right to judge!

Then, after an early dinner, we took off on our long

flight to Honolulu, with short stops at Guam and Wake. At last, with all official and social engagements behind me, I felt I was really on my way home. My first contact with the mainland of the United States was in Honolulu, when I was informed that New York City was calling me. I was petrified, as one always is, with the thought that something had gone wrong at home, but it was only a matter of a business question which my son John wanted to ask me. To him, Honolulu meant I was practically home, and therefore within telephone-calling distance.

Once I reach my own country after a trip I always want to get all the way home as fast as possible. I have experienced this feeling on every trip I have made, and it is exactly the way I felt on the last lap of this one. Consequently I decided not to linger on the coast, even though there were family and friends I wanted to see. I had a special reason for hurrying back this time, for Queen Juliana of the Netherlands was coming for a week end at Hyde Park, and I felt it was important to be there at least a few days before she arrived. I had been away for five months, with the exception of a few days over Christmas, and a house that has been empty that long can acquire a very deserted look.

By Way of Conclusion

It is curious how quickly when you are back in your own surroundings you slip into the rut of the day's routine and almost forget that only lately you have been completely immersed in the problems and interests of faraway countries. But I found after this trip that I could not forget some of the things I had seen and experienced and felt; they remained with me still. The excitement of meeting the dedicated people who are building a new world in Israel, and the interest of my first acquaintance with the Middle East in the Arab countries, the sense there of groping for better understanding, the pleasure and warmth of the contacts in Pakistan and India—all were unforgettable experiences.

When I try to gather my impressions and relate them to the world situation and to what may happen to the United States in the next few years, the touchstone seems always to be China—where I have never been. I think that in the past, most people who thought about Asia thought of China, because of her great size and population, as the heart of Asia, and felt that there was no other Eastern country whose healthy development would so profoundly affect the entire Asian continent. The United States always counted on a friendly relationship with her people. Much money was invested and many good people devoted themselves to ameliorating the life of her four hundred millions. Yet in the long run we failed to obtain the objectives we sought for the Chinese people.

There has been much argument about how it happened, and whether this policy or that policy was right or wrong, but for whatever reason, China is now in the hands of the Communists, and her leaders are undoubtedly close to their masters in the Kremlin. There are people in Asia, in Europe and even in this country who hope that China will prove to be more a socialist than a communist state, and that some of the objectionable features of Russian communism, which permit no individual freedom and smother everyone under a pall of fear, may be eliminated. These same people feel that communism has taken a more moderate form in Yugoslavia and that the people there are more influential with Tito, dictator though he is, than they were with Stalin or are with their present Russian masters. This is a difference important enough, they believe, to give us hope that these states may develop a type of communism that more nearly resembles socialism and with which it may be possible for the other countries of the world to live in peace.

Whatever pattern China follows, I should never want to see the United States or the United Nations engaged in a war with her. The vastness of the country and the size of her population would, in my opinion, make it a most unprofitable undertaking. In any case, I feel that the Chinese people have a right to develop their government along whatever lines they see fit.

If China can in time satisfactorily fulfill the qualifications of "a peace-loving state" I imagine she will eventually be admitted to the United Nations; and I hope that trade and diplomatic relations can then be restored. As long as the United Nations is at war in Korea, however, I see no possibility of any peaceful solution of our differences.

This makes India of greater importance than ever before. Already most of the countries of Asia look to her for leadership. Geographically, she lies between the Far East and Europe. On the strength of these facts alone, no country is in a better position to foster the growth of good will and understanding between East and West. Nowhere could the United Nations and the United States find more knowledgeable help in securing the best results from their aid programs in Asia. If India and Pakistan can be helped to solve their differences and surmount their internal difficulties, they will by their example be the most powerful sales argument the democracies of the West can offer to the people of the East.

We have a better chance in India than we had in China. In China much of the government was corrupt and the reforms that should have been made and that might have welded the people together under Chiang's leadership were not achieved. In India the government is honest and is straining every sinew to make the changes that will give the people a better life.

The statesmen of India know, I think, that the next few years will probably tell the story—whether the new government will be able to meet the needs of the people, to sustain their hopes and to give them a feeling that something is being accomplished, or whether the people, feeling that the change is not coming fast enough, will become discouraged and turn for help to some outside force that offers different methods and glibly promises quick and easy results.

It seems to me there is one thing our experience in China should bring home to us. Whether the Chinese Communists were Communists from the start and under Russian influence, or were merely agrarian reformers, as many people in the United States first thought, the conditions that drove them to seek a change were the all-important factor in the sequence of further events. In both India and Pakistan we should now look for the conditions that must be remedied if the same thing is not to happen there, and we must find better solutions than we found in China. Otherwise we may fail.

Chester Bowles, in every report to Congress and in every speech I heard him make and in every conversation, stressed the fact that economic aid is essential if we expect India— and I would add Pakistan—to develop strong and stable governments and achieve tangible results for the benefit of the people. Everything I myself saw and heard bears this out. Only tangible results can keep the Communist appeal from attracting the young people, the intellectuals, the farmers or the industrial workers, who in their hopelessness will feel they must try more drastic methods.

For the United Nations this means greater expense for all the countries that are working together in India and Pakistan.

For the United States it means a careful consideration of our policies in all parts of the world. We have felt, and rightly, I think, that it was necessary to build up our armed strength to the point where it would be impossible for Russia not to realize that Communist aggression anywhere in the world would be met by prompt resistance and punishment. This is costly, and brings us only one return: it gives us time to build up our economy and to help other nations to build up theirs.

We hear quite frequently in this country the cry that we cannot afford to put so much money into armaments and into the development of the atom bomb and at the same time to give so much in economic aid to the peoples of other countries. We can always get money for arms from Congress; but though it has been generous with relief and rehabilitation appropriations, it is not so easily convinced that economic aid is essential. Yet in the long run it may be more important than the money we spend for defense.

The same people who criticized our policy in China criticize the proposed policy in India. The very people who voted for national defense spending and want to cut down on plans for technical assistance are the people who once voted to give arms to Chiang Kai-shek and voted against economic aid to the Chinese people. They voted also against giving economic aid to the Republic of South Korea; and yet they are among those who are most violently critical of the results in South Korea and China. If the same policy of spending for defense but not for economic improvement is followed we will create in India the very situation which we today deplore in China and South Korea.

Even if it means sacrifice for the next few years, which are the crucial years for the world, it is essential that we pick the areas of the world where economic aid is primarily important and see to it that we do not fail the governments of those countries. I myself am convinced that India and Pakistan are the critical areas at the moment.

We have done much for Europe. We cannot completely and abruptly withdraw, particularly since that front is the one nearest to us. But I think we can find less expensive ways to stimulate European economic well-being. For one thing we should not follow the short-sighted policy of setting up tariff barriers against European goods just at the time when our best way of helping those countries to recover and to become strong lies in trading with them.

Trade is also an essential factor in the help we can give to the underdeveloped nations of the world at this time, for we can strongly bolster their economies by buying their raw materials. I think we will have to put some of our wisest, best trained and most astute people throughout the whole of the Eastern and Asiatic regions. Our policies and the friendship that we build up could tip the balance in favor of democracy and against communism.

We need every agency of the UN at work. We must call on science for the improvement of health and agriculture and for the better care of children. UNESCO must develop educational, programs so that people will be able to communicate with each other and understand each other's ends and means.

Above all, if the heavy burden our people and the people of other nations are now carrying is ever to be lifted, we must keep hammering at the Soviet government in the Disarmament Conference to try to bring it to some reasonable solution, so that less money need be spent on arms and more can be devoted to economic well-being.

One word I think I must say about the role that needs to be played by the citizens of the United States. Somehow we must be able to show people that democracy is not words, but action.

One of the things that is particularly impairing our leadership in many areas of the world is our treatment of minorities in our own country. Everywhere a traveler from the United States is asked whether what these people have heard about us is true. Sometimes they recite some incident they have heard or read about and ask whether this represents our idea of democracy. The Soviets see to it that the sordid stories of discrimination are known throughout the world; it is therefore important that we should tell the story of our efforts to improve human relations in this country and of our many successes. We must, of course, tell the truth and acknowledge our failures, but we should constantly cite examples showing that we are continually planning and striving for a more perfect democracy.

We must show by our behavior that we believe in equality and justice and that our religion teaches faith and love and charity to our fellow men. Here is where each of us has a job to do that must be done at home, because we can lose the battle on the soil of the United States just as surely as we can lose it in any one of the other countries of the world.

I said in the beginning of my book that I went out to the Middle East and to Asia to get an insight into the people and their problems. I believe that I did gain some understanding, and I would be happy to think that I helped some of them to a better understanding of us.

I shall never cease to hope that I may awaken in others a sense of the importance of these nations to the future of the world and a realization that we have strong potential friends there. We shall have to be willing to learn and to accept differences of opinion and background, for they will not always think and feel as we do, nor will they always accept our solutions to their problems. But if we try to understand them, they will, I think, come to understand us and to believe in us, and in our genuine desire to help them. For in the end we all want the same thing. We all want peace.

In the United Nations we are making an effort to work out the technique of living in harmony; and I have come to feel with ever-increasing conviction that work with and through the United Nations is the keystone to success in developing co-operation among countries and to peace in the future.

Index

Abraham, 35
Administrative inefficiency, 15
Afghanistan, 53, 92, 97
Afghan wars, 92, 93, 95
Afridi tribesmen, 93, 94
Agra, India, 168-71
Agriculture, India, 119-20; Indonesia, 213; Israel, 43; Lebanon, 5-6, 19; Nepal, 210; Pakistan, 79-80; Syria, 9
Ajanta Caves, 167-68
Akbar, 168
Aleppo, Syria, 18
Alexander the Great, 92
Ali, Mohammed, 72 n.
Aligarh, India, 176
Aligarh Moslem University, 176
Ali Khan, Begum Liaquat, 50, 63-65, 67, 68, 85, 90
Ali Khan, Mir Osman, 161-62
Allahabad, India, 179-91, 202
Allahabad University, 183-91
Alliance Tire and Rubber Company, 43
All-India Women's Conference, 116, 144, 163
All Pakistan Women's Association, 50, 57, 66, 67
Amber, India, 173
American University, Beirut, 19-20, 26-27
Amman, Jordan, 35
Anderson, Dr. Richmond K., 157
Arabian Sea, 154

Arab-Jewish riots, 26
Arab League, 34, 37
Arab refugees, 24-34
Aryans, 211
Assam, 56
Assyrians, 3
Atal, Mr., 149, 172-73, 176
Aurangabad, India, 165-67
Aurangzeb, 170, 171

Baber, 54, 92, 168
Baghdad, 17
Bahr-el-Huleh, 40
Balfour, Lord, 25
Balfour Declaration, 25
Baluchistan, province of, 56, 66, 88-89
Bangalore, India, 157, 159, 161
Bangkok, 213
Baratz, Joseph, 44-45
Bataan, 216
Bay of Bengal, 154, 204
Beersheba, 41-42
Beirut, Lebanon, 2, 8-9, 10, 19-20, 27
Beit-ed-dine, 6
Bekaa, Syria, 18
Benares, India, 202-4, 208
Ben Gurion, David, 44, 48-49
Bunche, Dr. Ralph, 24
Bhakra, Nangal, India, 131
Bihar, India, 131
Bikram, Maharajadhira Tribhubana Bir, 210-11

Index

Bolitho, Hector, 63
Bombay, India, 101, 139-47
Bowles, Chester, 102, 112, 114, 115-17, 122, 175, 208, 224
Brahmans, 133
Buddhism, 212
Buddhist temples, Nepal, 212
Burnier, Mr., 202, 203

Calcutta, India, 204-7, 208, 212
Calvary, 36
Cape Comorin, 154
Caste system, 133-34, 137
Cauvery River, 156
Ceylon, 154
Chamundi Bull, 155
Chamundi Temple, 155
Chenab River, 81
Chiang Kai-shek, 223, 226
Children's villages, Israel, 47-48
China, 221-24
Chittagong, Pakistan, 51, 84
Church of the Holy Sepulchre, 36
Cochrane, Merle, 213
Coimbatore, India, 122
Colleges and universities, India, 157, 176, 183-92; Israel, 36; Lebanon, 19-20, 26-27; Pakistan, 66-67, 99; Syria, 18
Colombo Plan, 121
Comay, Michael, 39
Communal settlements, Israel, 43-46
Communism, 5, 10, 23, 100, 183-91, 192, 197-98, 200, 215, 222, 225
Congress, U. S., 225
Co-operative communities, Israel, 46

Corr, Maureen, 1, 39, 144, 173
Cornwallis, General, 158
Corregidor, 216

Damascus, 9, 10, 14, 17, 18
Dasappa, H. C., 155, 156, 157
Dead Sea, 35
Dewey, Admiral George, 217
Degania, Israel, 43
Discovery of India, Nehru, 106-8, 182
Djakarta, Indonesia, 213, 215
Dome of the Rock, 35

East Bengal, 56, 81, 82
East Punjab, 82
Economic aid, 225-26; see also Point Four program
Education, India, 153-54; Near East, 15; Pakistan, 69-70; Philippines, 218
Egyptians, 3
Electrification, Lebanon, 19
Ellora Caves, 166-67, 168
Etawah, India, 123-30, 131, 179

Faridabad, India, 132-33, 134
First World War, 4
Folk dancing, India, 137, 151; Pakistan, 74-75
Ford Foundation, 20, 62, 67, 80, 85, 121-22, 129, 200
Fort Ali Masjid, 95

Gandhi, Mohandas, 102, 117, 133, 134, 175, 176, 191, 192, 195-96
Ganges River, 81, 202-4
General Electric Company, 84
Genghis Khan, 54

Index

George VI, of England, 37
Ghosh, Sudhir, 132-33
Ghulam, Mohammed, 58, 78
Gideon, Mr., 39
Governmental standards, 15-16
Graham, Dr. Frank P., 53, 178-79
Greek influence, 3
Guam, 220
Gurewitsch, Dr. David, 1-2, 39, 96, 97, 144, 149, 156, 173, 188, 202

Hadera, Israel, 43
Haifa, Israel, 43
Hastings, Warren, 158
Hebrew University, 36, 37
Himalayas, 50, 131, 208, 212
Hinduism, 212
Hindu Kush, 53, 92, 94
Hindu-Moslem rivalry, 53-57
Hirakud, India, 131
Hittites, 3
Hoffman, Paul, 200-1
Holi carnival, 163, 172
Holmes, Horace, 123-25
Honolulu, 220
Hooghly River, 204
Hostility, Lebanon, 2-3
Housing projects, 14; India, 138; Israel, 42; Pakistan, 77-78, 85
Huleh swamps, Israel, 40
Hussain, Dr. Zakir, 176
Hutheesing, Raja, 147
Hyde Park, 220
Hyderabad, India, 161-65
Hyder Ali, 157-58

Illiteracy, 7-8
Immigrants, Israel, 27, 40-42, 47
Imperialism, American, 114

India, 101-207, 221, 223-24, 226; agriculture, 119-20; British influence, 159-61; British rule in, 54-55, 113; caste system, 133-34, 137; cattle, 126-127; colleges and universities, 122, 143, 157, 176, 183-92; communism, 192, 197-98, 200; democratic republic, 56 n.; democracy in, 111-12; education, 153-54; emancipation of women, 21; fertilizer, 132; Five Year Plan, 110, 119, 130, 153, 199; food situation, 118; housing, 138; independence, 110; international co-operation, 121-123; irrigation, 120-21, 130-32; Point Four aid, 114, 123, 130, 132, 154; political parties, 109-10; population, 118-19; power systems, 130-31; princely states, 52; quarrel with Pakistan, 52-57; refugees, 204; renunciation, 194-200; Russian propaganda, 206-7; sanitation, 127-28; self-government, 55; water problem, 120-21
Indian Civil Service, 61, 120, 173
Indian Constitution, 105, 134
Indian Ocean, 50, 154
Indonesia, 213-16
Indus River, 82-83
Industry, Israel, 42-43; Lebanon, 6, 9; Pakistan, 51, 83-84; Syria, 9
International Bank, 48, 79
Iran, 42
Irrigation, India, 120-21; 130-32; Israel, 38; Lebanon, 19; Pakistan, 51, 80-81

Index

Israel, 24, 27, 33-34, 113, 221;
agriculture, 43; children's villages, 47-48; communal settlements, 43-46; dedicated land,
35-49; diversity and elasticity,
46-47; financial crisis, 48;
housing, 42; immigrants, 27,
40-42, 47; industry, 42-43;
irrigation, 38; Point Four aid,
48; population, 38; reparations
from Germany, 48
Israel Development Corporation,
43-44
Israeli-Arab dispute, 22-34, 44-45

Jaipur, India, 171-75
Jamrud Fort, 93
Japan, Pakistan trade, 86-87
Java, 213-14
Jehan, Shah, 168, 169
Jericho, 35
Jerusalem, 12, 24, 35-38
Jesus of Nazareth, 36
Jhelum River, 81
Jinnah, Fatima, 62-63
Jinnah, Mohammed Ali, 62, 69
Johnson and Johnson, 84
John the Baptist, 35
Jordan, 9-10, 14, 29-30; Point
Four aid, 17; political back-
ground, 4; population, 23
Jordan River, 38, 40
Juliana, Queen of the Nether-
lands, 220
Jumma Masjid, mosque of, 159
Jumna River, 117

Kaiser-Frazer plant, 43
Karachi, Pakistan, 50, 51, 57-91,
92, 101, 103

Karnafuli, East Pakistan, 83
Kashmir, 52, 53, 82, 102, 179
Kathiawar Peninsula, 135
Katju, Dr., 179-80, 182, 194-95,
199
Katmandu, Nepal, 116, 208, 212
Kaur, Rajkumari Amrit, 102
Khan, Lady Zafrullah, 73-74
Khan, Sir Zafrullah, 73
Khoury, Bechara el, 13
Khyber Pass, 51-52, 53, 92-100,
151
Khyber Rifles, 93
King and I, The, 152
Kipling, Rudyard, 94
Knesset (Israeli parliament), 39
Koran, 68-69
Korea, 223, 226
Kotri Barrage, 80
Krishnarajsegar Dam, 155-56
Kshatriyas, 133

Lahore, Pakistan, 60, 65, 73, 78,
101
Lake Success, 25
Lake Tiberias, 45
League of Women Voters, 71
Lebanon, 2-9, 13-14; agriculture,
5-6, 19; American University
at Beirut, 19-20, 26-27; electrification, 19; hostility, 2-3;
illiteracy, 7-8; industry, 6, 9;
irrigation, 19; Point Four aid,
4-5, 19; political background,
3-4; population, 7; poverty, 5;
refugee camps, 28-29, 30-31;
refugees, 30; religious toleration, 23; water supplies, 19
Lebanon Parliament, 23
Lydda, Israel, 50

Index

Mahal, Mumtaz, 170
Mahmud of Ghazni, 53, 92
Malik, Begum Husain, 57-58, 62, 65
Malik, Dr. Charles, 1
Manila, P. I., 216-19
Mardan, Pakistan, 94
Mass evacuation, 32
Mecca, 36
Mehta, Hansa, 205
Menuhin, Yehudi, 143-44, 166
Meyer, Albert, 123
Minor, Harold, 12
Minority groups, 115, 227-28
Mitter, Lady, 205
Moab Mountains, 35
Modi, Governor, 124, 179
Mogul empire, 54
Mohammed, 36
Mohammedan religion, 21-24
Mongols, 211
Morocco, 42
Moslem influence, 3
Moslem invaders, 53-54
Mosque of Omar, 35
Mountbatten, Lady, 104-5
Mountbatten, Lord Louis, 56, 103, 105
Mount Everest, 212
Mount Scopus, 36, 37
Mutual Security Agency (MSA), 121
Mysore, India, 154-57
Mysore University, 157

National Congress Party, India, 55, 56, 108-9, 175
National Moslem League, India, 55
Nazimudden, Khwaja, 72-73, 78

Nebuchadnezzar, 35
Negev, 38, 40, 41
Nehru, Jawaharlal, 82, 90, 102, 105-10, 134, 176, 178, 179-80, 181-82, 185, 190, 198, 200-1, 207
Nepal, 208-12
Netherlands, 215
New Delhi, India, 101, 102-17, 134, 175-79, 196, 208
New Delhi University, 191
Noon, Lady Firoz Khan, 85
North-West Frontier Province, Pakistan, 56
North-West Frontier University, 99

Ording, Aak, xi

Pakistan, 50-91, 101-2, 113, 221, 223, 224, 226; agriculture, 79-80; army, 52; bridges and dams, 81; colleges and universities, 66-67, 99; education, 69-70; emancipation of women, 21, 57, 65-75; flow of rivers, 82; folk dancing, 74-75; government personnel, 61-62; health, 76-77; hospitals, 76-77, 78; housing, 77-78, 85; industry, 51, 83-84; irrigation, 51, 80-81; monogamy, trend toward, 68; partition, 51-52, 56; Point Four aid, 79-80; power developments, 83; purdah, custom, 68-74; quarrel with India, 52-57; refugees, 75-77; trade situation, 86-87; tribal discipline, 89

Index

Pandit, Madame Vijaya Lakshmi, 102, 144, 147, 176, 179-80, 185, 186, 187, 202
Paris, 1
Parsees, 142
Penrose, Dr. S. B. L., 20, 26-27
Persians, 3
Peshawar, Pakistan, 78, 92, 93, 95, 99
Pharaon, Henri, 14
Philippines, 216-19
Phoenicians, 3, 7, 8
Point Four program, 4-5, 17, 19, 20, 48, 79-80, 114, 121, 123, 130, 132, 154, 209
Population, India, 118-19; Israel, 38; Jordan, 23; Lebanon, 7; Syria, 23
Prasad, Rajenda, 103, 175, 178, 191
Proclamation of the State of Israel, 39
Punjab, 56, 60, 81, 95, 123
Purdah, custom of, 68-74

Quirino, President, 219

Rajghat, India, 117
Ram, Radha Sri, 202
Rangoon, 213
Rasul, Pakistan, 81, 83
Ravi River, 82
Red Cross, 29, 32, 105
Refugee camps, Lebanon, 28-29, 30-31
Refugees, Arab, 24-34; India, 204; Lebanon, 30; Pakistan, 75-77; Philippine, 217
Religious toleration, Lebanon, 23
Republic of China, 215

Republic of South Korea, 226
River, The, 175-76, 202
Rizal Stadium, Manila, 219
Rockefeller Foundation, 122
Rockefeller Foundation Research Institute, 157
Rock of the Ascension, 36
Roman influence, 3
Roosevelt, Franklin D., 58, 60, 71, 156
Roosevelt, James, 60
Roosevelt, John, 220
Roosevelt, Theodore, 140
Rose, Mr. and Mrs., 209-10
Rothschild-Hadassah Medical Center, 36

Saheb, Jam, of Nawanagar, 135-139
St. Thomas, 151-52
San Agustin, church of, 217
Santiniketan University, 191-92
Saudi Arabia, 40
Saurashtra, India, 135
Selenie, Syria, 18
Seringapatam, India, 157, 158
Sheba, Dr. Chain, 39
Shere Ali, 95
Sibi, Baluchistan, 66, 88-89
Sind, province of, 56
Sindri, India, 132
Singh, Jai, 171-72
Singh, Rani Maharaj, 144
Singh, Sir Hari, 93
Soekarno, President, 214
Solomon's Temple, 35
Soviet Union, 23, 206-7, 227
Spring, Lucy, 70
Spruance, Ambassador and Mrs., 216

Index

Stalin, Joseph, 222
Stanton, Edwin, 213
Sudras, 133
Sutlej River, 82, 131
Syria, 14; agriculture, 9; colleges, 18; constitution, 18, 21; industry, 9; land holdings, 18; Point Four aid, 17; political background, 4; population, 23

Tagore, Rabindranath, 191
Taj Mahal, 168, 169-71, 179
Tamerlane, 54
Tariff barriers, 226
Tata, Jamshedji, 142-43
Tata Institute of Social Sciences, 143
Thal Project, Punjab, 81
Tippoo Sahib, 157-58
Tito, Marshal, 222
Trade, 226-27
Trivandrum, India, 147-54
Tungabhadra River, 131
Tyler, Mr., American consul at Jerusalem, 37

Unemployment, 10
United Nations, 22, 24, 26, 27, 33, 52, 81, 214, 222, 223, 225, 227, 228; Arab Refugee Agency, 33; Committee on Human Rights, 1; Economic Commission for Asia and the Far East, 79; Educational, Social and Cultural Organization (UNESCO), 122, 154, 227;

Food and Agricultural Organization, 79, 122; International Children's Emergency Fund, 77, 116, 122; Relief and Works Agency for Palestine Refugees, 29; Technical Assistance program, 122
United States Information Service Center, 206
Untouchables, 133, 134

Vaisyas, 133
Velloidi, Mr., 163
Via Dolorosa, 36

Wailing Wall of the Jews, 35
Wake Island, 220
Warren, Avra, 80
Warsak, Pakistan, 83
Weizmann, Chaim, 25
Wellington, Duke of, 158
Wilson, Mr. and Mrs., 205-6
Women, emancipation, 20-21; India, 21; Pakistan, 57, 65-75; Philippine, 218
World Bank, 82
World Health Organization (WHO), 119, 121

Yemen, 40, 42
Yemenites, 40-41
Yen, James, 218
Youth Aliyah, 47
Yugoslavia, 222
Yunus Khan, Major, 102

Set in Linotype Electra
Format by Robert Cheney
Manufactured by The Haddon Craftsmen, Inc.
Published by HARPER & BROTHERS, New York

Prayer for a Departed Father and Mother

O GOD, our Heavenly Father, Who hast commanded us to honor our Father and our Mother, have mercy on the departed souls of my dear Father and Mother, and grant that, if they are not yet with Thee, they may soon come to enjoy Thy blessed vision in Heaven; through Jesus Christ our Lord. *Amen.*

Joe Kotcka

416A

DESIGN COPR. 1955 DEVOTIONAL PUBLISHING CO. LITHO IN U. S. A.